GREEK
TRAGEDIES

VOLUME

2

AESCHYLUS

THE LIBATION BEARERS
Translated by Richmond Lattimore

SOPHOCLES

ELECTRA
Translated by David Grene

EURIPIDES

IPHIGENIA IN TAURIS
Translated by Witter Bynner

ELECTRA
Translated by Emily Townsend Vermeule

THE TROJAN WOMEN
Translated by Richmond Lattimore

GREEK TRAGEDIES

Edited by

DAVID GRENE *and* RICHMOND LATTIMORE

VOLUME

2

THE UNIVERSITY OF CHICAGO PRESS

CHICAGO & LONDON

THE UNIVERSITY OF CHICAGO PRESS, CHICAGO 60637
The University of Chicago Press, Ltd., London

Published 1960 by The University of Chicago Press
Printed in the United States of America
88 87 86 85 84 83 82 81   12 13 14 15

International Standard Book Number: 0–226–30775–1
Library of Congress Catalog Card Number: 60–950

NOTE

For this selection from *The Complete Greek Tragedies*, the University of Chicago Press has asked me to write the introductions. Longer and fuller introductions, mostly by the translators themselves, will be found in *The Complete Greek Tragedies*. As befits a limited volume, I have tried to state, very briefly, the essential features of each tragedy here reprinted. The personal views given are, of course, my own, and the translators, other than myself, are not to be held responsible.

R. L.

CONTENTS

THE LIBATION BEARERS

Translated by Richmond Lattimore

INTRODUCTION

The Libation Bearers is the second tragedy in *The Oresteia* (*Agamemnon*, *The Libation Bearers*, *The Eumenides*), which was produced in 458 B.C.

The dramatic time is some ten years after *Agamemnon*. Clytaemestra and Aegisthus rule in Argos, oppressing Electra, the daughter of Clytaemestra and Agamemnon, who hates them. Orestes, her brother, Agamemnon's son, has grown up in exile. He returns, is recognized by Electra, and with her plots, and himself carries out, the murder of Clytaemestra and Aegisthus.

Sophocles in his *Electra* and Euripides in his *Electra* told the same story. The important features special to Aeschylus are as follows. The recognition is begun through identification, by Electra, of her brother's hair, deposited on Agamemnon's tomb, and his footprints. The two children, with the chorus of Clytaemestra's slave women, speak and chant a long invocation to the spirit of Agamemnon and the gods of the earth, working themselves up to an act of which they sense the horror. Electra then leaves the stage, does not reappear, and takes no further part in the action. Aegisthus is killed first, off stage, and Orestes confronts Clytaemestra before the audience, then forces her inside the palace and kills her there. At the end, Orestes cannot enjoy his triumph. As he stands over the corpses, justifying his act, the horror comes on him and his mind sees the Furies of his mother, the Eumenides, who pursue him from the stage. The story of this pursuit and the release of Orestes is told in *The Eumenides*.

All three dramatists have made the murders accomplished by deception. Orestes presents himself disguised and is not recognized at first by his mother and her husband. In Aeschylus, the intrigue is reduced to its simplest terms. Much of the tragedy's force comes from the spellbinding rhythms and imagery of the invocation and the choral odes.

NOTE

The translation of this play is based on H. W. Smyth's "Loeb Classical Library" text (London and New York: William Heinemann, Ltd., and G. P. Putnam's Sons, 1926). A few deviations from this text occur where the translator has followed the manuscript readings instead of emendations accepted by Smyth.

Various editions of Greek drama divide the lines of lyric passages in various ways, but editors regularly follow the traditional line numbers whether their own line divisions tally with these numbers or not. This accounts for what may appear to be erratic line numbering in this translation. The line numbering in this translation is that of Smyth's text.

CHARACTERS

Orestes, son of Agamemnon and Clytaemestra

Pylades, his friend

Electra, his sister

Chorus, of foreign serving-women

A servant (doorkeeper)

Clytaemestra, now wife of Aegisthus, queen of Argos

Cilissa, the nurse

Aegisthus, now king of Argos

A follower of Aegisthus

Various attendants of Orestes, Clytaemestra, Aegisthus (silent parts)

THE LIBATION BEARERS

SCENE: *Argos. The first part of the play (1–651) takes place at the tomb of Agamemnon: the last part (652 to the end) before the door of Clytaemestra's palace. No mechanical change of scene is necessary. The altar or tomb of Agamemnon should be well down stage. The door to the house should be in the center, back.*

(*Enter, as travelers, Orestes and Pylades.*)

Orestes

Hermes, lord of the dead, who watch over the powers
of my fathers, be my savior and stand by my claim.
Here is my own soil that I walk. I have come home;
and by this mounded gravebank I invoke my sire
to hear, to listen.   5
Here is a lock of hair for Inachus, who made
me grow to manhood. Here a strand to mark my grief.
I was not by, my father, to mourn for your death
nor stretched my hand out when they took your corpse away.

(*The chorus, with Electra, enter from the side.*)

But what can this mean that I see, this group that comes   10
of women veiled in dignities of black? At what
sudden occurrence can I guess? Is this some new
wound struck into our house? I think they bring these urns
to pour, in my father's honor, to appease the powers
below. Can I be right? Surely, I think I see   15
Electra, my own sister, walk in bitter show
of mourning. Zeus, Zeus, grant me vengeance for my father's
murder. Stand and fight beside me, of your grace.

Pylades, stand we out of their way. So may I learn
the meaning of these women; what their prayer would ask.   20

Chorus

I came in haste out of the house
to carry libations, hurt by the hard stroke of hands.

« 5 »

My cheek shows bright, ripped in the bloody furrows
of nails gashing the skin.   25
This is my life: to feed the heart on hard-drawn breath.
And in my grief, with splitting weft
of ragtorn linen across my heart's
brave show of robes
came sound of my hands' strokes   30
in sorrows whence smiles are fled.

Terror, the dream diviner of
this house, belled clear, shuddered the skin, blew wrath
from sleep, a cry in night's obscure watches,
a voice of fear deep in the house,   35
dropping deadweight in women's inner chambers.
And they who read the dream meanings
and spoke under guarantee of God
told how under earth
dead men held a grudge still   40
and smoldered at their murderers.

On such grace without grace, evil's turning aside
(Earth, Earth, kind mother!)
bent, the godless woman   45
sends me forth. But terror
is on me for this word let fall.
What can wash off the blood once spilled upon the ground?
O hearth soaked in sorrow,
o wreckage of a fallen house.   50
Sunless and where men fear to walk
the mists huddle upon this house
where the high lords have perished.

The pride not to be warred with, fought with, not to be beaten
    down   55
of old, sounded in all men's
ears, in all hearts sounded,
has shrunk away. A man
goes in fear. High fortune,

this in man's eyes is god and more than god is this.   60
But, as a beam balances, so
sudden disasters wait, to strike
some in the brightness, some in gloom
of half dark in their elder time.
Desperate night holds others.   65

Through too much glut of blood drunk by our fostering ground
the vengeful gore is caked and hard, will not drain through.
The deep-run ruin carries away
the man of guilt. Swarming infection boils within.   70

For one who handles the bridal close, there is no cure.
All the world's waters running in a single drift
may try to wash blood from the hand
of the stained man; they only bring new blood guilt on.   75

But as for me: gods have forced on my city
resisted fate. From our fathers' houses
they led us here, to take the lot of slaves.
And mine it is to wrench my will, and consent
to their commands, right or wrong,   80
to beat down my edged hate.
And yet under veils I weep
the vanities that have killed
my lord; and freeze with sorrow in the secret heart.

Electra

Attendant women, who order our house, since you
are with me in this supplication and escort   85
me here, be also my advisers in this rite.
What shall I say, as I pour out these outpourings
of sorrow? How say the good word, how make my prayer
to my father? Shall I say I bring it to the man
beloved, from a loving wife, and mean my mother? I   90
have not the daring to say this, nor know what else
to say, as I pour this liquid on my father's tomb.
Shall I say this sentence, regular in human use:

"Grant good return to those who send to you these flowers
of honor: gifts to match the . . . evil they have done."   95

Or, quiet and dishonored, as my father died
shall I pour out this offering for the ground to drink,
and go, like one who empties garbage out of doors,
and turn my eyes, and throw the vessel far away.

Dear friends, in this deliberation stay with me.   100
We hold a common hatred in this house. Do not
for fear of any, hide your thought inside your heart.
The day of destiny waits for the free man as well
as for the man enslaved beneath an alien hand.
If you know any better course than mine, tell me.   105

Chorus

In reverence for your father's tomb as if it were
an altar, I will speak my heart's thought, as you ask.

Electra

Tell me then, please, as you respect my father's grave.

Chorus

Say words of grace for those of good will, as you pour.

Electra

Whom of those closest to me can I call my friend?   110

Chorus

Yourself first; all who hate Aegisthus after that.

Electra

You mean these prayers shall be for you, and for myself?

Chorus

You see it now; but it is you whose thought this is.

Electra

Is there some other we should bring in on our side?

Chorus

Remember Orestes, though he wanders far away.   115

Electra

That was well spoken; you did well reminding me.

Chorus

Remember, too, the murderers, and against them . . .

Electra

What shall I say? Guide and instruct my ignorance.

Chorus

Invoke the coming of some man, or more than man.

Electra

To come to judge them, or to give them punishment?   120

Chorus

Say simply: "one to kill them, for the life they took."

Electra

I can ask this, and not be wrong in the gods' eyes?

Chorus

May you not hurt your enemy, when he struck first?

Electra

Almighty herald of the world above, the world
below: Hermes, lord of the dead, help me; announce
my prayers to the charmed spirits underground, who watch   125
over my father's house, that they may hear. Tell Earth
herself, who brings all things to birth, who gives them strength,
then gathers their big yield into herself at last.
I myself pour these lustral waters to the dead,
and speak, and call upon my father: Pity me;   130
pity your own Orestes. How shall we be lords
in our house? We have been sold, and go as wanderers
because our mother bought herself, for us, a man,
Aegisthus, he who helped her hand to cut you down.
Now I am what a slave is, and Orestes lives   135
outcast from his great properties, while they go proud
in the high style and luxury of what you worked

to win. By some good fortune let Orestes come
back home. Such is my prayer, my father. Hear me; hear.
And for myself, grant that I be more temperate   140
of heart than my mother; that I act with purer hand.

Such are my prayers for us; but for our enemies,
father, I pray that your avenger come, that they
who killed you shall be killed in turn, as they deserve.
Between my prayer for good and prayer for good I set   145
this prayer for evil; and I speak it against Them.
For us, bring blessings up into the world. Let Earth
and conquering Justice, and all gods beside, give aid.

Such are my prayers; and over them I pour these drink
offerings. Yours the strain now, yours to make them flower   150
with mourning song, and incantation for the dead.

Chorus

Let the tear fall, that clashes as it dies
as died our fallen lord;
die on this mound that fences good from evil,
washing away the death stain accursed   155
of drink offerings shed. Hear me, oh hear, my lord,
majesty hear me from your dark heart; oh hear.
Let one come, in strength
of spear, some man at arms who will set free the house   160
holding the Scythian bow backbent in his hands,
a barbarous god of war spattering arrows
or closing to slash, with sword hilted fast to his hand.

Electra

Father, the earth has drunk my offerings poured to you.
Something has happened here, my women. Help me now.   165

Chorus

Speak, if you will. My heart is in a dance of fear.

Electra

Someone has cut a strand of hair and laid it on
the tomb.

Chorus

What man? Or was it some deep-waisted girl?

Electra

There is a mark, which makes it plain for any to guess.   170

Chorus

Explain, and let your youth instruct my elder age.

Electra

No one could have cut off this strand, except myself.

Chorus

Those others, whom it would have become, are full of hate.

Electra

Yet here it is, and for appearance matches well . . .

Chorus

With whose hair? Tell me. This is what I long to know. . . .   175

Electra

With my own hair. It is almost exactly like.

Chorus

Can it then be a secret gift from Orestes?

Electra

It seems that it must be nobody's hair but his.

Chorus

Did Orestes dare to come back here? How could this be?

Electra

He sent this severed strand, to do my father grace.   180

Chorus

It will not stop my tears if you are right. You mean
that he can never again set foot upon this land.

Electra

The bitter wash has surged upon my heart as well.
I am struck through, as by the cross-stab of a sword,

and from my eyes the thirsty and unguarded drops   185
burst in a storm of tears like winter rain, as I
look on this strand of hair. How could I think some other
man, some burgess, could ever go grand in hair like this?
She never could have cut it, she who murdered him
and is my mother, but no mother in her heart   190
which has assumed God's hate and hates her children. No.
And yet, how can I say in open outright confidence
this is a treasured token from the best beloved
of men to me, Orestes? Does hope fawn on me?
Ah
I wish it had the kind voice of a messenger   195
so that my mind would not be torn in two, I not
shaken, but it could tell me plain to throw this strand
away as vile, if it was cut from a hated head,
or like a brother could have mourned with me, and been
a treasured splendor for my father, and his grave.   200

The gods know, and we call upon the gods; they know
how we are spun in circles like seafarers, in
what storms. But if we are to win, and our ship live,
from one small seed could burgeon an enormous tree.

But see, here is another sign. Footprints are here.   205
The feet that made them are alike, and look like mine.
There are two sets of footprints: of the man who gave
his hair, and one who shared the road with him. I step
where he has stepped, and heelmarks, and the space between
his heel and toe are like the prints I make. Oh, this   210
is torment, and my wits are going.

(*Orestes comes from his place of concealment.*)

Orestes

    Pray for what is to come, and tell the gods that they
    have brought your former prayers to pass. Pray for success.

Electra

    Upon what ground? What have I won yet from the gods?

Orestes

You have come in sight of all you long since prayed to see.   215

Electra

How did you know what man was subject of my prayer?

Orestes

I know about Orestes, how he stirred your heart.

Electra

Yes; but how am I given an answer to my prayers?

Orestes

Look at me. Look for no one closer to you than I.

Electra

Is this some net of treachery, friend, you catch me in?   220

Orestes

Then I must be contriving plots against myself.

Electra

It is your pleasure to laugh at my unhappiness.

Orestes

I only mock my own then, if I laugh at you.

Electra

Are you really Orestes? Can I call you by that name?

Orestes

You see my actual self and are slow to learn. And yet   225
you saw this strand of hair I cut in sign of grief
and shuddered with excitement, for you thought you saw
me, and again when you were measuring my tracks.
Now lay the severed strand against where it was cut
and see how well your brother's hair matches my head.   230
Look at this piece of weaving, the work of your hand
with its blade strokes and figured design of beasts. No, no,
control yourself, and do not lose your head for joy.
I know those nearest to us hate us bitterly.

Electra

O dearest, treasured darling of my father's house,   235
hope of the seed of our salvation, wept for, trust
your strength of hand, and win your father's house again.
O bright beloved presence, you bring back four lives
to me. To call you father is constraint of fact,
and all the love I could have borne my mother turns   240
your way, while she is loathed as she deserves; my love
for a pitilessly slaughtered sister turns to you.
And now you were my steadfast brother after all.
You alone bring me honor; but let Force, and Right,
and Zeus almighty, third with them, be on your side.   245

Orestes

Zeus, Zeus, direct all that we try to do. Behold
the orphaned children of the eagle-father, now
that he has died entangled in the binding coils
of the deadly viper, and the young he left behind
are worn with hunger of starvation, not full grown   250
to bring their shelter slain food, as their father did.
I, with my sister, whom I name, Electra here,
stand in your sight, children whose father is lost. We both
are driven from the house that should be ours. If you
destroy these fledgelings of a father who gave you   255
sacrifice and high honor, from what hand like his
shall you be given the sacred feast which is your right?
Destroy the eagle's brood, and you have no more means
to send your signs to mortals for their strong belief;
nor, if the stump rot through on this baronial tree,   260
shall it sustain your altars on sacrificial days.
Safe keep it: from a little thing you can raise up
a house to grandeur, though it now seem overthrown.

Chorus

O children, silence! Saviors of your father's house,
be silent, children. Otherwise someone may hear   265
and for mere love of gossip carry news of all

you do, to those in power, to those I long to see
some day as corpses in the leaking pitch and flame.

Orestes

The big strength of Apollo's oracle will not
forsake me. For he charged me to win through this hazard,   270
with divination of much, and speech articulate,
the winters of disaster under the warm heart
were I to fail against my father's murderers;
told me to cut them down in their own fashion, turn
to the bull's fury in the loss of my estates.   275
He said that else I must myself pay penalty
with my own life, and suffer much sad punishment;
spoke of the angers that come out of the ground from those
beneath who turn against men; spoke of sicknesses,
ulcers that ride upon the flesh, and cling, and with   280
wild teeth eat away the natural tissue, how on this
disease shall grow in turn a leprous fur. He spoke
of other ways again by which the avengers might
attack, brought to fulfilment from my father's blood.
For the dark arrow of the dead men underground   285
from those within my blood who fell and turn to call
upon me; madness and empty terror in the night
on one who sees clear and whose eyes move in the dark,
must tear him loose and shake him until, with all his bulk
degraded by the bronze-loaded lash, he lose his city.   290
And such as he can have no share in the communal bowl
allowed them, no cup filled for friends to drink. The wrath
of the father comes unseen on them to drive them back
from altars. None can take them in nor shelter them.
Dishonored and unloved by all the man must die   295
at last, shrunken and wasted away in painful death.

Shall I not trust such oracles as this? Or if
I do not trust them, here is work that must be done.
Here numerous desires converge to drive me on:
the god's urgency and my father's passion, and   300

with these the loss of my estates wears hard on me;
the thought that these my citizens, most high renowned
of men, who toppled Troy in show of courage, must
go subject to this brace of women; since his heart
is female; or, if it be not, that soon will show.   305

Chorus

Almighty Destinies, by the will
of Zeus let these things
be done, in the turning of Justice.
For the word of hatred spoken, let hate
be a word fulfilled. The spirit of Right   310
cries out aloud and extracts atonement
due: blood stroke for the stroke of blood
shall be paid. Who acts, shall endure. So speaks
the voice of the age-old wisdom.

Orestes

Father, o my dread father, what thing   315
can I say, can I accomplish
from this far place where I stand, to mark
and reach you there in your chamber
with light that will match your dark?
Yet it is called an action   320
of grace to mourn in style for the house,
once great, of the sons of Atreus.

Chorus

Child, when the fire burns
and tears with teeth at the dead man
it can not wear out the heart of will.   325
He shows his wrath in the after-
days. One dies, and is dirged.
Light falls on the man who killed him.
He is hunted down by the deathsong
for sires slain and for fathers,   330
disturbed, and stern, and enormous.

Electra

Hear me, my father; hear in turn
all the tears of my sorrows.
Two children stand at your tomb to sing
the burden of your death chant.   335
Your grave is shelter to suppliants,
shelter to the outdriven.
What here is good; what escape from grief?
Can we outwrestle disaster?

Chorus

Yet from such as this the god, if he will,   340
can work out strains that are fairer.
For dirges chanted over the grave
the winner's song in the lordly house;
bring home to new arms the beloved.

Orestes

If only at Ilium,   345
father, and by some Lycian's hands
you had gone down at the spear's stroke,
you would have left high fame in your house,
in the going forth of your children
eyes' admiration;   350
founded the deep piled bank of earth
for grave by the doubled water
with light lift for your household;

Chorus

loved then by those he loved
down there beneath the ground   355
who died as heroes, he would have held
state, and a lord's majesty,
vassal only to those most great,
the Kings of the under darkness.
For he was King on earth when he lived   360
over those whose hands held power of life
and death, and the staff of authority.

Electra

    No, but not under Troy's
    ramparts, father, should you have died,
    nor, with the rest of the spearstruck hordes   365
    have found your grave by Scamandrus' crossing.
    Sooner, his murderers
    should have been killed, as he was,
    by those they loved, and have found their death,
    and men remote from this outrage   370
    had heard the distant story.

Chorus

    Child, child, you are dreaming, since dreaming is a light
    pastime, of fortune more golden than gold
    or the Blessed Ones north of the North Wind.
    But the stroke of the twofold lash is pounding   375
    close, and powers gather under ground
    to give aid. The hands of those who are lords
    are unclean, and these are accursed.
    Power grows on the side of the children.

Orestes

    This cry has come to your ear   380
    like a deep driven arrow.
    Zeus, Zeus, force up from below
    ground the delayed destruction
    on the hard heart and the daring
    hand, for the right of our fathers.   385

Chorus

    May I claim right to close the deathsong
    chanted in glory across
    the man speared and the woman
    dying. Why darken what deep within me forever
    flitters? Long since against the heart's   390
    stem a bitter wind has blown
    thin anger and burdened hatred.

Electra

> May Zeus, from all shoulder's strength,
> pound down his fist upon them, 395
> ohay, smash their heads.
> Let the land once more believe.
> There has been wrong done. I ask for right.
> Hear me, Earth. Hear me, grandeurs of Darkness.

Chorus

> It is but law that when the red drops have been spilled 400
> upon the ground they cry aloud for fresh
> blood. For the death act calls out on Fury
> to bring out of those who were slain before
> new ruin on ruin accomplished.

Orestes

> Hear me, you lordships of the world below. 405
> Behold in assembled power, curses come from the dead,
> behold the last of the sons of Atreus, foundering
> lost, without future, cast
> from house and right. O god, where shall we turn?

Chorus

> The heart jumped in me once again 410
> to hear this unhappy prayer.
> I was disconsolate then
> and the deep heart within
> darkened to hear you speak it.
> But when strength came back hope lifted 415
> me again, and the sorrow
> was gone and the light was on me.

Electra

> Of what thing can we speak, and strike more close,
> than of the sorrows they who bore us have given?
> So let her fawn if she likes. It softens not. 420
> For we are bloody like the wolf
> and savage born from the savage mother.

Chorus

    I struck my breast in the stroke-style of the Arian,
    the Cissian mourning woman,
    and the hail-beat of the drifting fists was there to see   425
    as the rising pace went in a pattern of blows
    downward and upward until the crashing strokes
    played on my hammered, my all-stricken head.

Electra

    O cruel, cruel
    all daring mother, in cruel processional   430
    with all his citizens gone,
    with all sorrow for him forgotten
    you dared bury your unbewept lord.

Orestes

    O all unworthy of him, that you tell me.
    Shall she not pay for this dishonor   435
    for all the immortals,
    for all my own hands can do?
    Let me but take her life and die for it.

Chorus

    Know then, they hobbled him beneath the armpits,
    with his own hands. She wrought so, in his burial   440
    to make his death a burden
    beyond your strength to carry.
    The mutilation of your father. Hear it.

Electra

    You tell of how my father was murdered. Meanwhile I   445
    stood apart, dishonored, nothing worth,
    in the dark corner, as you would kennel a vicious dog,
    and burst in an outrush of tears, that came that day
    where smiles would not, and hid the streaming of my grief.
    Hear such, and carve the letters of it on your heart.   450

Chorus

Let words such as these
drip deep in your ears, but on a quiet heart.
So far all stands as it stands;
what is to come, yourself burn to know.
You must be hard, give no ground, to win home.   455

Orestes

I speak to you. Be with those you love, my father.

Electra

And I, all in my tears, ask with him.

Chorus

We gather into murmurous revolt. Hear
us, hear. Come back into the light.
Be with us against those we hate.   460

Orestes

Warstrength shall collide with warstrength; right with right.

Electra

O gods, be just in what you bring to pass.

Chorus

My flesh crawls as I listen to them pray.
The day of doom has waited long.
They call for it. It may come.   465

O pain grown into the race
and blood-dripping stroke
and grinding cry of disaster,
moaning and impossible weight to bear.
Sickness that fights all remedy.   470

Here in the house there lies
the cure for this, not to be brought
from outside, never from others
but in themselves, through the fierce wreck and bloodshed.
Here is a song sung to the gods beneath us.   475

Hear then, you blessed ones under the ground,
and answer these prayers with strength on our side,
free gift for your children's conquest.

Orestes

Father, o King who died no kingly death, I ask
the gift of lordship at your hands, to rule your house. 480

Electra

I too, my father, ask of you such grace as this:
to murder Aegisthus with strong hand, and then go free.

Orestes

So shall your memory have the feasts that men honor
in custom. Otherwise when feasts are gay, and portions
burn for the earth, you shall be there, and none give heed. 485

Electra

I too out of my own full dowership shall bring
libations for my bridal from my father's house.
Of all tombs, yours shall be the lordliest in my eyes.

Orestes

O Earth, let my father emerge to watch me fight.

Electra

Persephone, grant still the wonder of success. 490

Orestes

Think of that bath, father, where you were stripped of life.

Electra

Think of the casting net that they contrived for you.

Orestes

They caught you like a beast in toils no bronzesmith made.

Electra

Rather, hid you in shrouds that were thought out in shame.

Orestes

Will you not waken, father, to these challenges? 495

Electra

Will you not rear upright that best beloved head?

Orestes

Send out your right to battle on the side of those
you love, or give us holds like those they caught you in.
For they threw you. Would you not see them thrown in turn?

Electra

Hear one more cry, father, from me. It is my last.   500
Your nestlings huddle suppliant at your tomb: look forth
and pity them, female with the male strain alike.
Do not wipe out this seed of the Pelopidae.
So, though you died, you shall not yet be dead, for when
a man dies, children are the voice of his salvation   505
afterward. Like corks upon the net, these hold
the drenched and flaxen meshes, and they will not drown.
Hear us, then. Our complaints are for your sake, and if
you honor this our argument, you save yourself.

Chorus

None can find fault with the length of this discourse you drew   510
out, to show honor to a grave and fate unwept
before. The rest is action. Since your heart is set
that way, now you must strike and prove your destiny.

Orestes

So. But I am not wandering from my strict course
when I ask why she sent these libations, for what cause   515
she acknowledges, too late, a crime for which there is
no cure. Here was a wretched grace brought to a man
dead and unfeeling. This I fail to understand.
The offerings are too small for the act done. Pour out
all your possessions to atone one act of blood,   520
you waste your work, it is all useless, reason says.
Explain me this, for I would learn it, if you know.

Chorus

    I know, child, I was there. It was the dreams she had.
    The godless woman had been shaken in the night
    by floating terrors, when she sent these offerings.   525

Orestes

    Do you know the dream, too? Can you tell it to me right?

Chorus

    She told me herself. She dreamed she gave birth to a snake.

Orestes

    What is the end of the story then? What is the point?

Chorus

    She laid it swathed for sleep as if it were a child.

Orestes

    A little monster. Did it want some kind of food?   530

Chorus

    She herself, in the dream, gave it her breast to suck.

Orestes

    How was her nipple not torn by such a beastly thing?

Chorus

    It was. The creature drew in blood along with the milk.

Orestes

    No void dream this. It is the vision of a man.

Chorus

    She woke screaming out of her sleep, shaky with fear,   535
    as torches kindled all about the house, out of
    the blind dark that had been on them, to comfort the queen.
    So now she sends these mourning offerings to be poured
    and hopes they are medicinal for her disease.

Orestes

    But I pray to the earth and to my father's grave   540
    that this dream is for me and that I will succeed.

See, I divine it, and it coheres all in one piece.
If this snake came out of the same place whence I came,
if she wrapped it in robes, as she wrapped me, and if
its jaws gaped wide around the breast that suckled me,   545
and if it stained the intimate milk with an outburst
of blood, so that for fright and pain she cried aloud,
it follows then, that as she nursed this hideous thing
of prophecy, she must be cruelly murdered. I
turn snake to kill her. This is what the dream portends.   550

Chorus

I choose you my interpreter to read these dreams.
So may it happen. Now you must rehearse your side
in their parts. For some, this means the parts they must not play.

Orestes

Simple to tell them. My sister here must go inside.
I charge her to keep secret what we have agreed,   555
so that, as they by treachery killed a man of high
degree, by treachery tangled in the self same net
they too shall die, in the way Loxias has ordained,
my lord Apollo, whose word was never false before.
Disguised as an outlander, for which I have all gear,   560
I shall go to the outer gates with Pylades
whom you see here. He is hereditary friend
and companion-in-arms of my house. We two shall both assume
the Parnassian dialect and imitate the way
they talk in Phocis. If none at the door will take us in   565
kindly, because the house is in a curse of ills,
we shall stay there, till anybody who goes by
the house will wonder why we are shut out, and say:
"why does Aegisthus keep the suppliant turned away
from his gates, if he is hereabouts and knows of this?"   570
But if I once cross the doorstone of the outer gates
and find my man seated upon my father's throne,
or if he comes down to confront me, and uplifts
his eyes to mine, then lets them drop again, be sure,

before he can say: "where does the stranger come from?" I   575
shall plunge my sword with lightning speed, and drop him dead.
Our Fury who is never starved for blood shall drink
for the third time a cupful of unwatered blood.

Electra, keep a careful eye on all within
the house, so that our plans will hold together. You,   580
women: I charge you, hold your tongues religiously.
Be silent if you must, or speak in the way that will
help us. And now I call upon the god who stands
close, to look on, and guide the actions of my sword.

            (*Exeunt Orestes and Pylades. Exit separately, Electra.*)

Chorus

Numberless, the earth breeds   585
dangers, and the sober thought of fear.
The bending sea's arms swarm
with bitter, savage beasts.
Torches blossom to burn along
the high space between ground and sky.   590
Things fly, and things walk the earth.
Remember too
the storm and wrath of the whirlwind.

But who can recount all
the high daring in the will   595
of man, and in the stubborn hearts of women
the all-adventurous passions
that couple with man's overthrow.
The female force, the desperate
love crams its resisted way   600
on marriage and the dark embrace
of brute beasts, of mortal men.

Let him, who goes not on flimsy wings
of thought, learn from her,
Althaea, Thestius'
daughter: who maimed her child, and hard   605
of heart, in deliberate guile

set fire to the bloody torch, her own son's
agemate, that from the day he emerged
from the mother's womb crying
shared the measure of all his life   610
down to the marked death day.

And in the legends there is one more, a girl
of blood, figure of hate
who, for the enemy's   615
sake killed one near in blood, seduced by the wrought
golden necklace from Crete,
wherewith Minos bribed her. She sundered
from Nisus his immortal hair
as he all unsuspecting   620
breathed in a tranquil sleep. Foul wretch,
Hermes of death has got her now.

Since I recall cruelties from quarrels long
ago, in vain, and married love turned to bitterness
a house would fend far away   625
by curse; the guile, treacheries of the woman's heart
against a lord armored in
power, a lord his enemies revered,
I prize the hearth not inflamed within the house,
the woman's right pushed not into daring.   630

Of all foul things legends tell the Lemnian
outranks, a vile wizard's charm, detestable
so that man names a hideous
crime "Lemnian" in memory of their wickedness.
When once the gods loathe a breed   635
of men they go outcast and forgotten.
No man respects what the gods have turned against.
What of these tales I gather has no meaning?

The sword edges near the lungs.
It stabs deep, bittersharp,   640
and right drives it. For that which had no right

lies not yet stamped into the ground, although
one in sin transgressed Zeus' majesty.   645

Right's anvil stands staunch on the ground
and the smith, Destiny, hammers out the sword.
Delayed in glory, pensive from
the murk, Vengeance brings home at last   650
a child, to wipe out the stain of blood shed long ago.

                                        (*Enter Orestes and Pylades.*)
Orestes

In there! Inside! Does anyone hear me knocking at
the gate? I will try again. Is anyone at home?
Try a third time. I ask for someone to come from the house,   655
if Aegisthus lets it welcome friendly visitors.

Servant (*inside*)

All right, I hear you. Where does the stranger come from, then?

Orestes

Announce me to the masters of the house. It is
to them I come, and I have news for them to hear.
And be quick, for the darkening chariot of night   660
leans to its course; the hour for wayfarers to drop
anchor in some place that entertains all travelers.
Have someone of authority in the house come out,
the lady of the place or, more appropriately,
its lord, for then no delicacy in speaking blurs   665
the spoken word. A man takes courage and speaks out
to another man, and makes clear everything he means.

                                        (*Enter Clytaemestra.*)
Clytaemestra

Friends, tell me only what you would have, and it is yours.
We have all comforts that go with a house like ours,
hot baths, and beds to charm away your weariness   670
with rest, and the regard of temperate eyes. But if
you have some higher business, more a matter of state,
that is the men's concern, and I will tell them of it.

Orestes

I am a Daulian stranger out of Phocis. As
I traveled with my pack and my own following   675
making for Argos, where my feet are rested now,
I met a man I did not know, nor did he know
me, but he asked what way I took, and told me his.
It was a Phocian, Strophius; for he told me his name
and said: "Friend, since in any case you make for Argos,   680
remember carefully to tell Orestes' parents
that he is dead; please do not let it slip your mind.
Then, if his people decide to have him brought back home,
or bury him where he went to live, all outlander
forever, carry their requests again to me.   685
For as it is the bronze walls of an urn close in
the ashes of a man who has been deeply mourned."

So much I know, no more. But whether I now talk
with those who have authority and concern in this
I do not know. I think his father should be told.   690

Clytaemestra

Ah me. You tell us how we are stormed from head to heel.
Oh curse upon our house, bitter antagonist,
how far your eyes range. What was clean out of your way
your archery brings down with a distant deadly shot
to strip unhappy me of all I ever loved.   695
Even Orestes now! He was so well advised
to keep his foot clear of this swamp of death. But now
set down as traitor the hope that was our healer once
and made us look for a bright revel in our house.

Orestes

I could have wished, with hosts so prosperous as you,   700
to have made myself known by some more gracious news
and so been entertained by you. For what is there
more kindly than the feeling between host and guest?
Yet it had been abuse of duty in my heart

had I not given so great a matter to his friends,   705
being so bound by promise and the stranger's rights.

Clytaemestra

You shall not find that your reception falls below
your worth, nor be any the less our friend for this.
Some other would have brought the news in any case.
But it is the hour for travelers who all day have trudged   710
the long road, to be given the rest that they deserve.
Escort this gentleman with his companion and
his men, to where our masculine friends are made at home.
Look after them, in manner worthy of a house
like ours; you are responsible for their good care.   715
Meanwhile, we shall communicate these matters to
the masters of the house, and with our numerous friends
deliberate the issues of this fatal news.

                                                    (*Exeunt all but the Chorus.*)

Chorus

Handmaidens of this house, who help our cause,
how can our lips frame   720
some force that will show for Orestes?
O Lady Earth, Earth Queen, who now
ride mounded over the lord of ships
where the King's corpse lies buried,
hear us, help us.   725
Now the time breaks for Persuasion in stealth
to go down to the pit, with Hermes of death
and the dark, to direct
trial by the sword's fierce edge.

I think our newcomer is at his deadly work;   730
I see Orestes' old nurse coming forth, in tears.

                                                    (*Enter Cilissa.*)

Now where away, Cilissa, through the castle gates,
with sorrow as your hireless fellow-wayfarer?

Cilissa

The woman who is our mistress told me to make haste
and summon Aegisthus for the strangers, "so that he   735
can come and hear, as man to man, in more detail
this news that they have brought." She put a sad face on
before the servants, to hide the smile inside her eyes
over this work that has been done so happily
for her—though on this house the curse is now complete   740
from the plain story that the stranger men have brought.
But as for that Aegisthus, oh, he will be pleased
enough to hear the story. Poor unhappy me,
all my long-standing mixture of misfortunes, hard
burden enough, here in this house of Atreus,   745
when it befell me made the heart ache in my breast.
But never yet did I have to bear a hurt like this.
I took the other troubles bravely as they came:
but now, darling Orestes! I wore out my life
for him. I took him from his mother, brought him up.   750
There were times when he screamed at night and woke me from
my rest; I had to do many hard tasks, and now
useless; a baby is like a beast, it does not think
but you have to nurse it, do you not, the way it wants.
For the child still in swaddling clothes can not tell us   755
if he is hungry or thirsty, if he needs to make
water. Children's young insides are a law to themselves.
I needed second sight for this, and many a time
I think I missed, and had to wash the baby's clothes.
The nurse and laundrywoman had a combined duty   760
and that was I. I was skilled in both handicrafts,
and so Orestes' father gave him to my charge.
And now, unhappy, I am told that he is dead
and go to take the story to that man who has
defiled our house; he will be glad to hear such news.   765

Chorus

Did she say he should come back armed in any way?

Cilissa

How, armed? Say it again. I do not understand.

Chorus

Was he to come with bodyguards, or by himself?

Cilissa

She said to bring his followers, the men-at-arms.

Chorus

Now, if you hate our master, do not tell him that,   770
but simply bid him come as quickly as he can
and cheerfully. In that way he will not take fright.
It is the messenger who makes the bent word straight.

Cilissa

But are you happy over what I have told you?

Chorus

Perhaps: if Zeus might turn our evil wind to good.   775

Cilissa

How so? Orestes, once hope of the house, is gone.

Chorus

Not yet. It would be a poor seer who saw it thus.

Cilissa

What is this? Have you some news that has not been told?

Chorus

Go on and take your message, do as you were bid.
The gods' concerns are what concern only the gods.   780

Cilissa

I will go then and do all this as you have told
me to. May all be for the best. So grant us god.

(*Exit Cilissa.*)

Chorus

Now to my supplication, Zeus,
father of Olympian gods,

grant that those who struggle hard to see   785
temperate things done in the house win their aim
in full. All that I spoke
was spoken in right. Yours, Zeus, to protect.

Zeus, Zeus, make him who is now
in the house stand above those who   790
hate. If you rear him to greatness,
double and three times
and blithely he will repay you.

See the colt of this man whom you loved
harnessed to the chariot   795
of suffering. Set upon the race he runs
sure control. Make us not see him break
stride, but clean down the course
hold the strain of his striding speed.

You that, deep in the house   800
sway their secret pride of wealth,
hear us, gods of sympathy.
For things done in time past
wash out the blood in fair-spoken verdict.
Let the old murder in   805
the house breed no more.

And you, who keep, magnificent, the hallowed and huge
cavern, o grant that the man's house lift up its head
and look on the shining of daylight
and liberty with eyes made
glad with gazing out from the helm of darkness.   810

And with right may the son
of Maia lend his hand, strong to send
wind fair for action, if he will.
Much else lies secret he may show at need.   815
He speaks the markless word, by
night hoods darkness on the eyes
nor shows more plainly when the day is there.

Then at last we shall sing
for deliverance of the house   820
the woman's song that sets the wind
fair, no thin drawn and grief
struck wail, but this: "The ship sails fair."
My way, mine, the advantage piles here, with wreck
and ruin far from those I love.   825

Be not fear struck when your turn comes in the action
but with a great cry *Father*
when she cries *Child* to you
go on through with the innocent murder.   830

Yours to raise high within
your body the heart of Perseus
and for those under the ground you loved
and those yet above, exact
what their bitter passion may desire; make   835
disaster a thing of blood inside the house;
wipe out the man stained with murder.

                                            (*Enter Aegisthus.*)

Aegisthus

It is not without summons that I come, but called
by messenger, with news that there are strangers here
arrived, telling a story that brings no delight: 840
the death of Orestes. For our house, already bitten
and poisoned, to take this new load upon itself
would be a thing of dripping fear and blood. Yet how
shall I pass upon these rumors? As the living truth?
For messages made out of women's terror leap   845
high in the upward air and empty die. Do *you*
know anything of this by which to clear my mind?

Chorus

We heard, yes. But go on inside and hear it from
the strangers. Messengers are never quite so sure
as a man's questions answered by the men themselves.   850

Aegisthus

    I wish to question, carefully, this messenger
    and learn if he himself was by when the man died
    or if he heard but some blind rumor and so speaks.
    The mind has eyes, not to be easily deceived.

                             (Exit Aegisthus.)

Chorus

    Zeus, Zeus, what shall I say, where make   855
    a beginning of prayer for the gods' aid?
    My will is good
    but how shall I speak to match my need?
    The bloody edges of the knives that rip
    man-flesh are moving to work. It will mean   860
    utter and final ruin imposed
    on Agamemnon's
    house: or our man will kindle a flame
    and light of liberty, win the domain
    and huge treasure again of his fathers.   865
    Forlorn challenger, though blessed by god,
    Orestes must come to grips with two,
    so wrestle. Yet may he throw them.

              (A cry is heard from inside the house.)

    Listen, it goes   870
    but how? What has been done in the house?
    Stand we aside until the work is done, for so
    we shall not seem to be accountable in this
    foul business. For the fight is done, the issue drawn.

              (Enter a follower of Aegisthus.)

Follower

    O sorrow, all is sorrow for our stricken lord.   875
    Raise up again a triple cry of sorrow, for
    Aegisthus lives no longer. Open there, open
    quick as you may, and slide back the doorbars on the women's
    gates. It will take the strength of a young arm, but not
    to fight for one who is dead and done for. What use there?   880

Ahoy!
My cry is to the deaf and I babble in vain
at sleepers to no purpose. Clytaemestra, where
is she, does what? Her neck is on the razor's edge
and ripe for lopping, as she did to others before.

(*Enter Clytaemestra.*)

Clytaemestra

What is this, and why are you shouting in the house?   885

Follower

I tell you, he is alive and killing the dead.

Clytaemestra

Ah, so. You speak in riddles, but I read the rhyme.
We have been won with the treachery by which we slew.
Bring me quick, somebody, an ax to kill a man

(*Exit follower.*)

and we shall see if we can beat him before we   890
go down—so far gone are we in this wretched fight.

(*Enter Orestes and Pylades with swords drawn.*)

Orestes

You next: the other one in there has had enough.

Clytaemestra

Beloved, strong Aegisthus, are you dead indeed?

Orestes

You love your man, then? You shall lie in the same grave
with him, and never be unfaithful even in death.   895

Clytaemestra

Hold, my son. Oh take pity, child, before this breast
where many a time, a drowsing baby, you would feed
and with soft gums sucked in the milk that made you strong.

Orestes

What shall I do, Pylades? Be shamed to kill my mother?

Pylades

> What then becomes thereafter of the oracles   900
> declared by Loxias at Pytho? What of sworn oaths?
> Count all men hateful to you rather than the gods.

Orestes

> I judge that you win. Your advice is good.
>
>   (*To Clytaemestra.*)
>   Come here.
> My purpose is to kill you over his body.
> You thought him bigger than my father while he lived.   905
> Die then and sleep beside him, since he is the man
> you love, and he you should have loved got only your hate.

Clytaemestra

> I raised you when you were little. May I grow old with you?

Orestes

> You killed my father. Would you make your home with me?

Clytaemestra

> Destiny had some part in that, my child.

Orestes

>   Why then   910
> destiny has so wrought that this shall be your death.

Clytaemestra

> A mother has her curse, child. Are you not afraid?

Orestes

> No. You bore me and threw me away, to a hard life.

Clytaemestra

> I sent you to a friend's house. This was no throwing away.

Orestes

> I was born of a free father. You sold me.   915

Clytaemestra

> So? Where then is the price that I received for you?

Orestes

I could say. It would be indecent to tell you.

Clytaemestra

Or if you do, tell also your father's vanities.

Orestes

Blame him not. He suffered while you were sitting here at home.

Clytaemestra

It hurts women to be kept from their men, my child.   920

Orestes

The man's hard work supports the women who sit at home.

Clytaemestra

I think, child, that you mean to kill your mother.

Orestes
                                                 No.

It will be you who kill yourself. It will not be I.

Clytaemestra

Take care. Your mother's curse, like dogs, will drag you down.

Orestes

How shall I escape my father's curse, if I fail here?   925

Clytaemestra

I feel like one who wastes live tears upon a tomb.

Orestes

Yes, this is death, your wages for my father's fate.

Clytaemestra

You are the snake I gave birth to, and gave the breast.

Orestes

Indeed, the terror of your dreams saw things to come
clearly. You killed, and it was wrong. Now suffer wrong.   930

(*Orestes and Pylades take Clytaemestra inside the house.*)

Chorus

I have sorrow even for this pair in their twofold
downfall. But since Orestes had the hardiness
to end this chain of bloodlettings, here lies our choice,
that the eyes' light in this house shall not utterly die.

Justice came at the last to Priam and all his sons   935
and it was heavy and hard,
but into the house of Agamemnon returned
the double lion, the double assault,
and the Pythian-steered exile
drove home to the hilt   940
vengeance, moving strongly in guidance sent by the god.

Raise up the high cry o over our lordships' house
won free of distress, free of its fortunes wasted
by two stained with murder,
free of its mournful luck.   945

He came back; his work lay in the secret attack
and it was stealthy and hard
but in the fighting his hand was steered by the very daughter
of Zeus: Right we call her,
mortals who speak of her and name her well. Her wind   950
is fury and death visited upon those she hates.

All that Loxias, who on Parnassus holds
the huge, the deep cleft in the ground, shrilled aloud,
by guile that is no guile   955
returns now to assault the wrong done and grown old.
Divinity keeps, we know not how, strength to resist
surrender to the wicked.
The power that holds the sky's majesty wins our worship.   960

Light is here to behold.
The big bit that held our house is taken away.
Rise up, you halls, arise; for time grown too long
you lay tumbled along the ground.

Time brings all things to pass. Presently time shall cross 965
the outgates of the house after the stain is driven
entire from the hearth
by ceremonies that wash clean and cast out the furies.
The dice of fortune shall be thrown once more, and lie
in a fair fall smiling 970
up at the new indwellers come to live in the house.

*(The doors of the house open, to show Orestes standing over the
bodies of Clytaemestra and Aegisthus. His attendants display
the robe in which Clytaemestra had entangled Agamemnon and which she displayed after his murder.)*

Orestes

Behold the twin tyrannies of our land, these two
who killed my father and who sacked my house. For a time
they sat upon their thrones and kept their pride of state, 975
and they are lovers still. So may you judge by what
befell them, for as they were pledged their oath abides.
They swore together death for my unhappy sire
and swore to die together. Now they keep their oath.

Behold again, o audience of these evil things, 980
the engine against my wretched father they devised,
the hands' entanglement, the hobbles for his feet.
Spread it out. Stand around me in a circle and
display this net that caught a man. So shall, not my
father, but that great father who sees all, the Sun, 985
look on my mother's sacrilegious handiwork
and be a witness for me in my day of trial
how it was in all right that I achieved this death,
my mother's: for of Aegisthus' death I take no count:
he has his seducer's punishment, no more than law. 990

But she, who plotted this foul death against the man
by whom she carried the weight of children underneath
her zone, burden once loved, shown hard and hateful now,
what does she seem to be? Some water snake, some viper

whose touch is rot even to him who felt no fang   995
strike, by that brutal and wrong daring in her heart.

And this thing: what shall I call it and be right, in all
eloquence? Trap for an animal or winding sheet
for dead man? Or bath curtain? Since it is a net,
robe you could call it, to entangle a man's feet.   1000
Some highwayman might own a thing like this, to catch
the wayfarer and rob him of his money and
so make a living. With a treacherous thing like this
he could take many victims and go warm within.

May no such wife as she was come to live with me.   1005
Sooner, let God destroy me, with no children born.

Chorus

Ah, but the pitiful work.
Dismal the death that was your ending.
He is left alive; pain flowers for him.

Orestes

Did she do it or did she not? My witness is   1010
this great robe. It was thus she stained Aegisthus' sword.
Dip it and dip it again, the smear of blood conspires
with time to spoil the beauty of this precious thing.
Now I can praise him, now I can stand by to mourn
and speak before this web that killed my father; yet   1015
I grieve for the thing done, the death, and all our race.
I have won; but my victory is soiled, and has no pride.

Chorus

There is no mortal man who shall turn
unhurt his life's course to an end not marred.
There is trouble here. There is more to come.   1020

Orestes

I would have you know, I see not how this thing will end.
I am a charioteer whose course is wrenched outside
the track, for I am beaten, my rebellious senses

bolt with me headlong and the fear against my heart
is ready for the singing and dance of wrath. But while   1025
I hold some grip still on my wits, I say publicly
to my friends: I killed my mother not without some right.
My father's murder stained her, and the gods' disgust.
As for the spells that charmed me to such daring, I
give you in chief the seer of Pytho, Loxias. He   1030
declared I could do this and not be charged with wrong.
Of my evasion's punishment I will not speak:
no archery could hit such height of agony.
And look upon me now, how I go armored in
leafed branch and garland on my way to the centrestone   1035
and sanctuary, and Apollo's level place,
the shining of the fabulous fire that never dies,
to escape this blood that is my own. Loxias ordained
that I should turn me to no other shrine than this.
To all men of Argos in time to come I say   1040
they shall be witness, how these evil things were done.
I go, an outcast wanderer from this land, and leave
behind, in life, in death, the name of what I did.

Chorus

No, what you did was well done. Do not therefore bind
your mouth to foul speech. Keep no evil on your lips.   1045
You liberated all the Argive city when
you lopped the heads of these two snakes with one clean stroke.

Orestes

No!
Women who serve this house, they come like gorgons, they
wear robes of black, and they are wreathed in a tangle
of snakes. I can no longer stay.   1050

Chorus

Orestes, dearest to your father of all men
what fancies whirl you? Hold, do not give way to fear.

Orestes

These are no fancies of affliction. They are clear,
and real, and here; the bloodhounds of my mother's hate.

Chorus

It is the blood still wet upon your hands, that makes   1055
this shaken turbulence be thrown upon your sense.

Orestes

Ah, Lord Apollo, how they grow and multiply,
repulsive for the blood drops of their dripping eyes.

Chorus

There is one way to make you clean: let Loxias
touch you, and set you free from these disturbances.   1060

Orestes

You can not see them, but I see them. I am driven
from this place. I can stay here no longer.

                                                    (*Exit.*)

Chorus

Good luck go with you then, and may the god look on
you with favor and guard you in kind circumstance.

Here on this house of the kings the third   1065
storm has broken, with wind
from the inward race, and gone its course.
The children were eaten: there was the first
affliction, the curse of Thyestes.
Next came the royal death, when a man   1070
and lord of Achaean armies went down
killed in the bath. Third
is for the savior. He came. Shall I call
it that, or death? Where
is the end? Where shall the fury of fate   1075
be stilled to sleep, be done with?

                                                    (*Exeunt.*)

ELECTRA
Translated by David Grene

INTRODUCTION

There is no external evidence for the date of this play. Most scholars tend to put it late in the career of Sophocles, either on metrical grounds or because of the desire of a date close to that of Euripides' *Electra* (probably 413 B.C.). But there is no certainty.

As we have stated above, Sophocles' *Electra* tells the same story as *The Libation Bearers* of Aeschylus. That Sophocles' play is named after the heroine, rather than the hero or chorus, is not without significance. Electra does not disappear halfway through the action, as in Aeschylus; she is the main character; like Antigone, she is given a cautious sister to be a foil to her resolute spirit of resistance; and she is there at the end, cheering on her brother in his murderous work. Another clue to the spirit of the play is found in the instructions of Apollo, quoted by Orestes near the beginning (lines 37-38):

> "Take not spear nor shield nor host;
> go yourself, and craft of hand
> be yours to kill, with justice but with stealth."

For "stealth" we could even read "treachery." The deception is exploited. Orestes and his old retainer, the Paedagogus, concoct a story of how Orestes was killed in a racing accident at the Pythian Games; they bring on a funereal casket supposed to contain his ashes; we find, what is contrary to the normal practices of tragedy, a *false* messenger-speech; even Electra is deceived.

A final turn is given to the progress of the story by having Clytemnestra killed first. Any incipient feelings of remorse are swallowed in the need for instant action as the approach of Aegisthus is announced. The last lines spoken by Orestes can, again, be taken as a key (1507-8):

> Justice shall be taken
> directly on all who act above the law—
> justice by killing. So we would have less villains.

There are no Furies; there is no flight of Orestes. This is all—and critics are left to come to most various conclusions, including the conclusion that there is no conclusion. There is little lyric wonder, either in the speeches or in the choral odes. This is the liar's drama, without adornment except in the virtuosities of deception and punishment.

CHARACTERS

Paedagogus, the Old Servant Who Looked after Orestes when a Boy

Orestes, Son of Agamemnon, Murdered King of Mycenae

Electra, Daughter of Agamemnon

Chorus of Women of Mycenae

Chrysothemis, Sister of Electra

Clytemnestra, Widow of Agamemnon and Wife of Aegisthus

Aegisthus, Usurping King of Mycenae

ELECTRA

SCENE: *Before the royal palace in Mycenae.*

Paedagogus
> Son of Agamemnon, once general at Troy,
> now you are here, now you can see it all,
> all that your heart has always longed for.
> This is old Argos of your yearning, the grove
> of Inachus' gadfly-haunted daughter.
> And here, Orestes, is the Lycean market place
> of the wolf-killing God. Here on the left
> the famous temple of Hera. Where we have come now,
> believe your eyes, see golden Mycenae,
> and here the death-heavy house of the Pelopidae.   10
>
> Once on a time, your father's murder fresh,
> I took you from this house, received you from the hand
> of your sister, whose blood and father were yours.
> I saved you then. I have raised you from that day
> to this moment of your manhood to be the avenger
> of that father done to death. Orestes, now,
> and you, Pylades, dearest friend, take counsel
> quickly on what to do. Already the sunlight,
> brightening, stirs dawning bird song into clearness,
> and the black, kindly night of stars is gone.
> Before a man leaves his house, sets foot on the path,   20
> let us hold our parley. We are where
> we must not shrink. It is high time for action.

Orestes
> Dearest of servants:
> very plain are the signs you show of your nobility
> toward me. It is so with a horse of breeding.
> Even in old age, hard conditions
> do not break his spirit. His ears are still erect.

So it is with you. You urge me, and yourself
follow among the first. Therefore, I will make plain
all my determinations. Give keen ear   30
to what I say, and where I miss the mark
of what I should, correct me.

When I came to Pytho's place of prophecy
to learn to win revenge
for my father's murder on those that did that murder,
Phoebus spoke to me the words I tell you now:
"Take not spear nor shield nor host;
go yourself, and craft of hand
be yours to kill, with justice but with stealth."
Now we have heard the oracle together.
Go you into this house when occasion calls you.
Know all that is done there, and, knowing, report   40
clear news to us. You are old. It's a long time.
They will never know you. They will not suspect you
with your gray silver hair. Here is your story.
You are a stranger coming from Phanoteus,
their Phocian friend, the greatest of their allies.
Tell them a sudden accident befell
Orestes, and he's dead. Swear it on oath.
Say in the Pythian games he was rolled
out of his chariot at high speed.
That is your story now.   50

We shall go first to my father's grave
and crown it, as he bade us, with libations
and with cuttings from my thick, luxuriant hair.
And then we shall come here again
and in our hands a carved bronze-sided urn,
the urn that you know I hid here in the bushes.
By these means we shall bring the pleasant news
with our tale of lies, that here is my body,
quite gone to ashes, charred and burned, before them.

For why should it irk me if I die in word
but in deed come through alive and win my glory?   60
To my thinking, no word is base when spoken with profit.
Before now I have seen wise men often
dying empty deaths as far as words reported them,
and then, when they have come to their homes again,
they have been honored more, even to the skies.
So in my case I venture to predict
that I who die according to this rumor
shall, like a blazing star, glare on my foes again.

Land of my father, Gods of my country,
welcome me, grant me success in my coming,
and you, too, house of my father;
as your purifier I have come,
in justice sent by the Gods.   70
Do not send me dishonored out of this country,
but rich from of old time, restorer of my house.
This is all that I have to say. Old man,
let it be yours to go and mind your task.
We two must go away. It is seasonable,
and seasonableness is greatest master of every act.

Electra (*from inside the house cries out*)
  Ah! Ah!

Paedagogus
  Inside the house some one of the servants,
  I think, is crying.

Orestes
  Might it not be   80
  unfortunate Electra? Do you want us
  to stay here and to listen to her cries?

Paedagogus
  No. Nothing must come before we try
  to carry out what Loxias has bidden us.
  From there we must make our beginning,

pouring the lustral offerings for your father.
For that, I think, will bring us victory,
and mastery in our enterprise.

(*Orestes and his friends withdraw; Electra emerges.*)

Electra

O Holy Light
and air, copartner with light in earth's possession,
how many keening dirges,
how many plangent strokes
laid on the breast till the breast was bloody,   90
have you heard from me
when the darkling night withdrew?
And again in the house of my misery
my bed is witness to my all-night sorrowing
dirges for my unhappy father.
Him in the land of the foreigner
no murderous god of battles entertained.
But my mother and the man who shared her bed,
Aegisthus, split his head with a murderous ax,
like woodsmen with an oak tree.
For all this no pity was given him,   100
by any but me, no pity for your death,
father, so pitiful, so cruel.
But, for my part, I
will never cease my dirges and sorrowful laments,
as long as I have eyes to see
the twinkling light of the stars and this daylight.
So long, like a nightingale, robbed of her young,
here before the doors of what was my father's house
I shall cry out my sorrow for all the world to hear.

House of the Death God, house of Persephone,   110
Hermes of the Underworld, holy Curse,
Furies the Dread Ones, children of the Gods,
all ye who look upon those who die unjustly,
all ye who look upon the theft of a wife's love,

come all and help take vengeance for my father,
for my father's murder!
And send me my brother to my aid.
For alone to bear the burden I am no longer strong enough,
the burden of the grief that weighs against me.   120

Chorus

    Electra, child of the wretchedest of mothers,
    why with ceaseless lament do you waste away
    sorrowing for one long dead,
    Agamemnon, godlessly trapped
    by deceits of your treacherous mother,
    betrayed by her evil hand?
    May evil be the end
    of him that contrived the deed,
    if I may lawfully say it!

Electra

    True-hearted girls,
    you have come to console me in my troubles.   130
    I know, I understand what you say,
    nothing of it escapes me.
    But, all the same, I will not
    leave my mourning for my poor father.
    You whose love responds to mine in all ways,
    suffer me my madness,
    I entreat you.

Chorus

    But from the all-receptive lake
    of Death you shall not raise him,
    groan and pray as you will.
    If past the bounds of sense you dwell in grief   140
    that is cureless, with sorrow unending,
    you will only destroy yourself,
    in a matter where the evil knows no deliverance.
    It is only your discomfort.
    Why do you seek it?

Electra

Simple indeed is the one
that forgets parents pitifully dead.
Suited rather to my heart
the bird of mourning
that "Itys, Itys" ever does lament,
the bird of crazy sorrow, Zeus's messenger.
And Niobe, that suffered all, you, too,   150
I count God
who weeps perpetually
in her rocky grave.

Chorus

Not alone to you, my child,
this burden of grief has come.
You exceed in your feeling far
those of your kin and blood.
See the life of Chrysothemis
and Iphianassa,
and that one whose manhood grows in secret,
sorrowing, a prince,   160
whom one day this famed land of noble Mycenae
shall welcome back, if God will bless his coming,
Orestes.

Electra

I have awaited him always
sadly, unweariedly,
till I'm past childbearing,
till I am past marriage,
always to my own ruin.
Wet with tears, I endure
an unending doom of misfortune.
But he has forgotten
what he has suffered, what he has known.
What message comes from him to me
that is not again belied?   170

Yes, he is always longing to come,
but he does not choose to come, for all his longing.

Chorus

    Take heart, take heart, my child.
    Still great above is Zeus,
    who oversees all things in sovereign power.
    Confide to him your overbitter wrath.
    Chafe not overmuch against
    the foes you hate, nor yet forget them quite,
    for Time is a kindly God.
    For neither he that lives
    by Crisa's cattle-grazing shore,   180
    the son of Agamemnon, will be heedless,
    nor the God that rules by Acheron's waters.

Electra

    But for me already the most of my life
    has gone by without hope.
    And I have no strength any more.
    I am one wasted in childlessness,
    with no loving husband for champion.
    Like some dishonored foreigner,
    I tenant my father's house in these ugly rags   190
    and stand at a scanty table.

Chorus

    Pitiful was the cry at the homecoming,
    and pitiful, when on your father on his couch
    the sharp biting stroke of the brazen ax
    was driven home.
    Craft was the contriver, passion the killer,
    dreadfully begetting between them a Shape,
    dreadful, whether divine or human,
    was he that did this.   200

Electra

    That day of all days that have ever been
    most deeply my enemy.

O night, horrible burden
of that unspeakable banquet.
Shameful death that my father saw
dealt him by the hands of the two,
hands that took my own life captive,
betrayed, destroyed me utterly.
For these deeds may God in his greatness,
the Olympian one, grant punishment to match them.   210
And may they have no profit of their glory
who brought these actions to accomplishment.

Chorus

    Take heed you do not speak too far.
    Do you not see from what
    acts of yours you suffer as you do?
    To destruction self-inflicted
    you fall so shamefully.
    You have won for yourself
    superfluity of misfortune,
    breeding wars in your sullen soul
    evermore. You cannot fight
    such conflicts hand to hand, with mighty princes.   220

Electra

    Terrors compelled me,
    to terrors I was driven.
    I know it, I know my own spirit.
    With terrors around me, I will not hold back
    these mad cries of misery, so long as I live.
    For who, dear girls, who that thought right
    would believe there were suitable comforting
    words for me?
    Forbear, forbear, my comforters.
    These ills of mine shall be called cureless   230
    and never shall I give over my sorrow,
    and the number of my dirges none shall tell.

Chorus

    But only in good will to you I speak
    like some loyal mother, entreating
    not to breed sorrow from sorrow.

Electra

    What is the natural measure of my sorrow?
    Come, how when the dead are in question,
    can it be honorable to forget?
    In what human being is this instinctive?
    Never may I have honor of such,
    nor, if I dwell with any good thing,   240
    may I live at ease, by restraining
    the wings of shrill lament to my father's dishonor.
    For if he that is dead
    is earth and nothing,
    poorly lying,
    and they shall never in their turn
    pay death for death in justice,
    then shall all shame be dead
    and all men's piety.   250

Chorus

    My child, it was with both our interests at heart
    I came, both yours and mine. If what I say
    is wrong, have your own way. We will obey you.

Electra

    Women, I am ashamed if I appear
    to you too much the mourner with constant dirges.
    What I do, I must do. Pardon me. I ask you
    how else would any well-bred girl behave
    that saw her father's wrongs, as I have seen these,
    by day and night, always, on the increase
    and never a check?   260
    First there's my mother, yes, my mother, now become
    all hatred. Then in the house I live with those
    who murdered my father. I am their subject, and

whether I eat or go without depends
on them.

      What sort of days do you imagine
I spend, watching Aegisthus sitting
on my father's throne, watching him wear
my father's self-same robes, watching him
at the hearth where he killed him, pouring libations?   270
Watching the ultimate act of insult,
my father's murderer in my father's bed
with my wretched mother—if mother I should call her,
this woman that sleeps with him.
She is so daring that she paramours
this foul, polluted creature and fears no Fury.
No, as though laughing at what was done,
she has found out the day on which she killed
my father in her treachery, and on that day
has set a dancing festival and sacrifices   280
sheep, in monthly ritual, "to the Gods that saved her."
So within that house I see, to my wretchedness,
the accursed feast named in his honor.
I see it, moan, and waste away, lament—
but only to myself. I may not even cry
as much as my heart would have me.
For this woman, all nobility in words,
abuses me: "You hateful thing, God-hated,
are you the only one whose father is dead?
Is there no one else of human kind in mourning?   290
My curse upon you! May the Gods below
grant you from your present sorrows no release!"
Such is the tone of her insults, unless she hears
from someone of Orestes' coming. Then
she grows really wild and stands beside me shrieking:
"Are you too not responsible for this?
Is not this your doing, you who stole
Orestes from these hands of mine, conveying him
away? But you may be sure you will pay for it

and pay enough." She howls so, and nearby her
is her distinguished bridegroom, saying the same,   300
that utter dastard, mischief complete,
who makes his wars with women.
But I am waiting for Orestes' coming,
waiting forever for the one who will stop
all our wrongs. I wait and wait and die.
For his eternal going-to-do-something
destroys my hopes, possible and impossible.

In such a state, my friends, one cannot
be moderate and restrained nor pious either.
Evil is all around me, evil
is what I am compelled to practice.

Chorus
   Tell me, as you talk like this, is Aegisthus here,   310
   or is he gone from home?

Electra
   Certainly, he's gone.
   Do not imagine, if he were near, that I
   would wander outside. Now he is on his estate.

Chorus
   If so, I can talk with you with better heart.

Electra
   For the present, he is away. What do you want?

Chorus
   Tell me: what of your brother? Is he really coming
   or hesitating? That is what I want to know.

Electra
   He says he is—but does nothing of what he says.

Chorus
   A man often hesitates when he does a big thing.   320

Electra
   I did not hesitate when rescuing him.

Chorus

    Be easy.

    He's a true gentleman and will help his friends.

Electra

    I believe in him, or else had not lived so long.

Chorus

    Say no more now. I see your sister,

    blood of your blood, of the same father and mother,

    Chrysothemis, in her hands burial offerings,

    the usual sacrifice to the Gods below.

                     (Enter Chrysothemis, Electra's sister.)

Chrysothemis

    What have you come to say out of doors,

    sister? Will you never learn, in all this time,   330

    not to give way to your empty anger?

    Yet this much I know, and know my own heart, too,

    that I am sick at what I see, so that

    if I had strength, I would let them know how I feel.

    But under pain of punishment, I think,

    I must make my voyage with lowered sails,

    that I may not seem to do something and then prove

    ineffectual. But justice, justice,

    is not on my side but on yours. If I am

    to live and not as a prisoner, I must

    in all things listen to my lords.   340

Electra

    It is strange indeed that you who were born

    of our father should forget him

    and heed your mother. All these warnings

    of me you have learned from her. Nothing is your own.

    Now you must make your choice, one way or the other,

    either to be a fool

    or sensible—and to forget your friends.

    Here you are saying: "If I had the strength,

I would show my hatred of them!" You who, when I
did everything to take vengeance for my father,
never did a thing to help—yes, discouraged the doer.   350
Is not this cowardice on top of baseness?
Tell me, or let me tell you, what benefit
I would achieve by giving up my mourning?
Do I not live? Yes, I know, badly, but
for me enough. And I hurt them
and so give honor to the dead, if there is, there
in that other world, anything that brings pleasure.
But you who hate, you tell me, hate in word only
but in fact live with our father's murderers.

I tell you: never, not though they brought me your gifts
in which you now feel pride, would I yield to them.   360
Have your rich table and your abundant life.
All the food I need is the quiet of my conscience.
I do not want to win your honor.
nor would you if you were sound of mind. Now, when you could
be called the daughter of the best of fathers,
be called your mother's. Thus to most people prove base,
traitor to your dead father and your friends.

Chorus

    No anger, I entreat you. In the words of both
    there is value for both, if you, Electra, can   370
    follow her advice and she take yours.

Chrysothemis

    O ladies, I am used to her and her words.
    I never would have mentioned this, had not
    I learned of the greatest of misfortunes coming
    her way to put a stop to her long mourning.

Electra

    Tell me of your terror. If you can speak to me
    of something worse than this condition of mine,
    I'll not refuse it still.

Chrysothemis
Well, I shall tell you.
From what I learned—and if you don't give over
your present mourning—they will send you where   380
never a gleam of sun shall visit you.
You shall live out your life in an underground cave
and there bewail sorrows of the world outside.
With this in mind, reflect. And do not blame me
later when you are suffering.
Now is a good time to take thought.

Electra
So this is what they have decided to do with me.

Chrysothemis
Yes, this exactly, when Aegisthus comes home.

Electra
As far as this goes, let him come home soon.

Chrysothemis
Why such a prayer for evil, my poor darling?

Electra
That he may come—if he will do what you say.

Chrysothemis
Hoping that *what* may happen you? Are you crazy?   390

Electra
That I may get away from you all, as far as I can.

Chrysothemis
Have you no care of this, your present life?

Electra
Mine is indeed a fine life, to be envied.

Chrysothemis
It might be, if you could learn common sense.

Electra
Do not teach me falseness to those I love.

Chrysothemis
That, that is not what I teach, but to yield to authority.

Electra
Practice your flattery. This is not my way.

Chrysothemis
It is a good thing, though, not to fall through stupidity.

Electra
I shall fall, if I must, revenging my father.

Chrysothemis
My father will have pardon for me, I know. 400

Electra
These are words that the base may praise.

Chrysothemis
You will not heed me then? You will not agree?

Electra
No, certainly.
May I not yet be so empty-witted.

Chrysothemis
Then I must go on the errand I was bid.

Electra
Where are you going? To whom
bringing burnt offering?

Chrysothemis
My mother sent me with offerings for father's grave.

Electra
What are you saying? To her greatest enemy?

Chrysothemis
"Whom she has killed"—you would add.

Electra
Which of her friends persuaded her? Who thought of this?

Chrysothemis
I think it was night terrors drove her to it.

Electra
Gods of my father, now or never stand my friends!

Chrysothemis
Why do "night terrors" make you confident?

Electra
I'll tell you that when you tell me the dream.

Chrysothemis
I cannot tell you much, only a little.

Electra
Tell me it, all the same. Often this little
has made or ruined men.

Chrysothemis
There is a story that she saw my father,
the father that was yours and mine, again
coming to life, once more to live with her.
He took and at the hearth planted the scepter
which once he bore and now Aegisthus bears,
and up from out the scepter foliage sprang
luxuriantly, and shaded all the land
of this Mycenae. This is what I heard
from someone present when she told the Sun
the nature of her dreams.
                                        But beyond this
I know no more, only that she sends me
because of her fear. And, by the Gods, I pray you,
the Gods that live in this country, listen to me
and do not fall out of stupidity.
For if you should reject me, she will come
again to harry you with punishment.

Electra
My dear one, not a morsel that you hold
allow to touch that grave, no, nothing.

It would not be God's law nor pious that you
should offer to my father sacrifices
and lustral offerings from that enemy woman.
Throw them to the winds! Or hide them in deep hollowed
earth, somewhere where no particle of them
may ever reach my father where he lies.
But let them be stored up for her as treasures
below, against the day when *she* shall die.
I tell you, if she were not the most brazen   440
of all of womankind, would she have dared
to pour these enemy libations
over the body of the man she killed?
Consider if you think that the dead man,
as he lies in his grave, will welcome kindly
these offerings from her by whom he was robbed
of life and honor? By whom, mutilated?
And for her purification she wiped
the blood stains on his head? Can you believe
that these will prove for her a quittance offering?
No, no. You let them be. You cut a lock
out of your own hair, from the fringe and mine,
mine, too, his wretched daughter's. Such a small offering,   450
yet all I have! Give it to him, this lustrous
lock of hair, and here, my girdle, unadorned.
Kneel then and pray that from that nether world
he may come, a friendly spirit, to our help
against his enemies. Pray that the boy Orestes
may live to fight and win against his enemies,
may live to set his foot upon them.
                              And so
in days to come we shall be able to dress
this grave with richer hands than we can now.
I think, oh yes, I think that it was he
that thought to send this evil-boding dream   460
to her.
          Yet, sister, do yourself this service

and help me, too, and help the dearest of all,
our common father, that lies dead in the underworld.

Chorus
    The girl speaks well. And you, my dear,
    if you are wise, will follow her advice.

Chrysothemis
    I will do it. It is not reasonable for us two
    to squabble about what is just. We must haste to do something.
    But, my friends, if I attempt this, I must have your silence.
    If my mother hears of this, I am sure I shall rue   470
    indeed the attempt I shall make.

Chorus
    If I am not a distracted prophet
    and lacking in skill of judgment,
    Justice foreshadowing the event
    shall come, in her hands a just victory.
    Yes, she will come, my child, in vengeance
    and soon.
    Of that I was confident
    when I lately heard,   480
    of this dream of sweet savor.
    Your father, the king of the Greeks,
    has never forgotten,
    nor the ax of old,
    bronze-shod, double-toothed,
    which did him to death
    in shame and baseness.

    There shall come many-footed, many-handed,
    hidden in dreadful ambush,   490
    the bronze-shod Fury.
    Wicked indeed were they who were seized
    with a passion for a forbidden bed,
    for a marriage accursed, stained with murder.
    In the light of this, I am very sure

that never, never shall we see
such a portent draw near without hurt
to doers and partners in crime.
There are no prophecies for mortal men
in dreadful dreams and soothsayings
if this night vision come not,   500
well and truly to fulfilment.

Horsemanship of Pelops of old,
loaded with disaster,
how deadly you have proved
to this land!
For since the day that Myrtilus
fell asleep, sunk in the sea,
wrecked utterly with the unhappy
wreck of his golden carriage,   510
for never a moment since
has destruction and ruin
ever left this house.

(*Queen Clytemnestra enters from the palace.*)

Clytemnestra

It seems you are loose again, wandering about.
Aegisthus isn't here, who always restrains you
from going abroad and disgracing your family.
But now that he is away you pay no heed
to me, although there's many a one you have told   520
at length how brutally and how unjustly
I lord it over you, insulting
you and yours.
                        There is no insolence in myself,
but being abused by you so constantly
I give abuse again.
                        Your father, yes,
always your father. Nothing else is your pretext—
the death he got from me. From me. I know it,
well. There is no denial in me. Justice,

Justice it was that took him, not I alone.
You would have served the cause of Justice if
you had been right-minded.
For this your father whom you always mourn,   530
alone of all the Greeks, had the brutality
to sacrifice your sister to the Gods,
although he had not toiled for her as I did,
the mother that bore her, he the begetter only.
Tell me, now, why he sacrificed her. Was it
for the sake of the Greeks?

They had no share in my daughter to let them kill her.
Was it for Menelaus' sake, his brother,
that he killed my child? And shall he not then pay for it?
Had not this Menelaus two children who
ought to have died rather than mine? It was their parents   540
for whose sake all the Greeks set sail for Troy.
Or had the God of Death some longing to feast
on my children rather than hers? Or had
that accursed father lost the love of mine
and felt it still for Menelaus' children?
This was the act of a father thoughtless
or with bad thoughts. That is how I see it
even if you differ with me.
                              The dead girl,
if she could speak, would bear me out.
I am not dismayed by all that has happened.
If you think me wicked, keep your righteous judgment   550
and blame your neighbors.

Electra

This is one time you will not be able to say
that the abuse I receive from you was provoked
by something painful on my side.
                              But if
you will allow me I will speak truthfully
on behalf of the dead man and my dead sister.

Clytemnestra

    Of course, I allow you. If you had always begun
    our conversations so, you would not have been
    so painful to listen to.

Electra

                I will tell you, then.
    You say you killed my father. What claim more shameful
    than that, whether with justice or without it?   560
    But I'll maintain that it was not with justice
    you killed him, but the seduction of that bad man,
    with whom you now are living, drew you to it.
    Ask Artemis the Huntress what made her hold
    the many winds in check at Aulis. Or
    I'll tell you this. *You* dare not learn from her.

    My father, as I hear, when at his sport,
    started from his feet a horned dappled stag
    within the Goddess' sanctuary. He
    let fly and hit the deer and uttered some boast
    about his killing of it. The daughter of Leto   570
    was angry at this and therefore stayed the Greeks
    in order that my father, to compensate
    for the beast killed, might sacrifice his daughter.

    Thus was her sacrifice—no other deliverance
    for the army either homeward or toward Ilium.
    He struggled and fought against it. Finally,
    constrained, he killed her—not for Menelaus.
    But if—I will plead in your own words—he had done so
    for his brother's sake, is that any reason
    why he should die at your hands? By what law?
    If this is the law you lay down for men, take heed   580
    you do not lay down for yourself ruin and repentance.
    If we shall kill one in another's requital,
    you would be the first to die, if you met with justice.

No. Think if the whole is not a mere excuse.
Please tell me for what cause you now commit
the ugliest of acts—in sleeping with him,
the murderer with whom you first conspired
to kill my father, and breed children to him, and
your former honorable children born   590
of honorable wedlock you drive out.
What grounds for praise shall I find in this? Will you say
that this, too, is retribution for your daughter?
If you say it, still your act is scandalous.
It isn't decent to marry with your enemies
even for a daughter's sake.

                                    But I may not
even rebuke you! What you always say
is that it is my mother I am reviling.
Mother! I do not count you mother of mine,
but rather a mistress. My life is wretched
because I live with multitudes of sufferings,
inflicted by yourself and your bedfellow.   600
But the other, he is away, he has escaped
your hand, though barely. Sad Orestes now
wears out his life in misery and exile.
Many a time you have accused me
of rearing him to be your murderer.
I would have done it if I could. Know that.
As far as that goes, you may publicly
proclaim me what you like—traitor, reviler,
a creature full of shamelessness.

                                    If I am
naturally skilled as such, I do no shame
to the nature of the mother that brought me forth.

Chorus

>   I see she is angry, but whether it is in justice,   610
>   I no longer see how I shall think of that.

Clytemnestra

    What need have *I* of thought in her regard
    who so insults her mother, when a grown woman?
    Don't you think she will go to any lengths, so shameless
    as she is?

Electra

           You may be sure I am ashamed,
    although you do not think it. I know why
    I act so wrongly, so unlike myself.
    The hate you feel for me and what you do
    compel me against my will to act as I do.   620
    For ugly deeds are taught by ugly deeds.

Clytemnestra

    O vile and shameless, I and my words and deeds
    give you too much talk.

Electra

    It is you who talk, not I. It is your deeds,
    and it is deeds invent the words.

Clytemnestra

    Now by the Lady Artemis you shall not escape
    the results of your behavior, when Aegisthus comes.

Electra

    You see? You let me say what I please, and then
    you are outraged. You do not know how to listen.

Clytemnestra

    Hold your peace at least. Allow me sacrifice,   630
    since I have permitted you to say all you will.

Electra

    I allow you, yes, I bid you, sacrifice.
    Do not blame my lips; for I will say no more.

Clytemnestra (to the maid)

    Come, do you lift them up, the offerings

of all the fruits of earth, that to this King here
I may offer my prayers for freedom from my fears.

(She speaks to the image of Apollo.)

Phoebus Protector, hear me, as I am,
although the word I speak is muted. Not among friends
is it spoken, nor may I unfold the whole
to the light while this girl stands beside me,   640
lest with her chattering tongue, wagging in malice,
she sow in all the city bad reports.
Yet hear me as I speak. So I will put it:
the dreams of double meaning I have seen
within this night, for them, Lycaean King,
grant what is good in them prosperous issue
but what is ill, turn it again upon
those that do us ill.
If there are some that from my present wealth
plot to expel me with their stratagems,
do not permit them. Let me live out my life,   650
just as my life is now, to the end uninjured,
controlling the house of Atreus and the throne,
living with those I love as I do now,
the good days on our side, and with such children
as do not hate me nor cause bitter pain.
These are my prayers, Lycaean Apollo, hear them
graciously. Grant to all of us what we ask.
For all the rest, although I am silent,
I know you are a God and know it all.
It is natural that the children of Zeus see all.

(Enter Paedagogus.)

Paedagogus
    Foreign ladies, how may I know for certain,   660
    is this the palace of the King Aegisthus?

Chorus
    This is it, sir. Your own guess is correct.

Paedagogus
> Would I then be right in thinking this lady
> his wife? She has indeed a royal look.

Chorus
> Quite right. Here she is for you, herself.

Paedagogus
> Greetings, your Majesty. I come with news,
> pleasant news for you and Aegisthus and your friends.

Clytemnestra
> I welcome what you have said. I would like first
> to know who sent you here.

Paedagogus
> The Phocian,
> Phanoteus, charging me with a grave business.   670

Clytemnestra
> What is it, sir? Please tell me. I know well
> you come from a friend and will speak friendly words.

Paedagogus
> Orestes is dead. There it is, in one short word.

Electra
> O God, O God! This is the day I die.

Clytemnestra
> What is this you say, sir, what? Don't listen to her.

Paedagogus
> What I said and say now is "Orestes is dead."

Electra
> God help me, I am dead—I cannot live now.

Clytemnestra
> Leave her to herself. Sir, will you tell me the truth,
> in what way did he meet his death?

Paedagogus
> This
> I was sent to tell, and I will tell you it all.   680

He went to the glorious gathering that Greece holds
in honor of the Delphic Games, and when
he heard the herald's shrill proclamation
for the first contest—it was a running race—
he entered glorious, all men's eyes upon him.
His running was as good as his appearance.
He won the race and came out covered with honor.
There is much I could tell you, but I must tell it briefly.   690
I do not know a man of such achievement
or prowess. Know this one thing. In all the contests
the marshals announced, he won the prize, was cheered,
proclaimed the victor as "Argive by birth,
by name Orestes, son of the general
Agamemnon who once gathered the great Greek host."
So much for that. But when a God sends mischief,
not even the strong man may escape.

                       Orestes,
when, the next day, at sunset, there was a race
for chariot teams, entered with many contestants.   700
There was one Achaean, one from Sparta, two
Libyans, masters in driving racing teams.
Orestes was the fifth among them. He
had as his team Thessalian mares. The sixth
was an Aetolian with young sorrel horses.
The seventh was a Magnesian, and the eighth
an Aenean, by race, with a white team.
The ninth competitor came from God-built Athens,
and then a Boeotian, ten chariots in all.
They stood in their allotted stations where   710
the appointed judges placed them. At the signal,
a brazen trumpet, they were off. The drivers
cheered their horses on, their hands vibrating the reins,
all together. All the course was filled
with the noise of rattling chariots. Clouds of dust
rose up. The mass of drivers, huddled together,
did not spare the goad as each one struggled

to put the nave of his wheel or the snorting mouths
of his horses past his rival, wheels and backs
of the foremost drivers all beslobbered with foam,   720
as the breath of the teams behind beat on them.
So far all chariots were uninjured. Then
the Aenean's hard-mouthed colts got out of hand
and bolted as they finished the sixth lap
and turned into the seventh. There they crashed
head on with the Barcaean. After that,
from this one accident, team crashed team
and overset each other. All the plain
of Crisa was full of wrecks. But the man from Athens,   730
a clever driver, saw what was happening, pulled
his horses out of the way and held them in check,
letting past the disordered mass of teams in the middle.
Orestes had been driving last and holding
his horses back, putting his trust in the finish.
But when he saw the Athenian left alone,
he sent a shrill cry through his good horses' ears
and set to catch him. The two drove level,
the poles were even. First one, now the other,
would push his horses' heads in front.   740
Orestes always drove tight at the corners
barely grazing the edge of the post with his wheel,
loosing his hold of the trace horse on his right
while he checked the near horse. In his other laps
the poor young man and his horses had come through safe.
But this time he let go of the left rein
as the horse was turning. Unaware, he struck the edge
of the pillar and broke his axle in the center.
He was himself thrown from the rails of the chariot
and tangled in the reins. As he fell, the horses
bolted wildly to the middle of the course.
When the crowd saw him fallen from his car,
they shuddered. "How young he was," "How gallant his deeds,"   750
and "How sadly he has ended," as they saw him

thrown earthward now, and then, tossing his legs
to the sky—until at last the grooms
with difficulty stopped the runaway team
and freed him, but so covered with blood that no one
of his friends could recognize the unhappy corpse.
They burned him on the pyre. Then men of Phocis
chosen for the task have brought here in a small urn
the lamentable ashes—all that is left
of this great frame, that he may have his grave   760
here in his father's country.
                              That is my story,
bitter as stories go, but for us who saw it,
greatest of all ill luck these eyes beheld.

Chorus

    Woe, woe. The ancient family
    of our lords has perished, it seems, root and branch.

Clytemnestra

    Zeus, what shall I say? Shall I say "good luck"
    or "terrible, but for the best"? Indeed,
    my state is terrible if I must save
    my life by the misfortunes of myself.

Paedagogus

    My lady, why does this story make you dejected?

Clytemnestra

    Mother and child! It is a strange relation.   770
    A mother cannot hate the child she bore
    even when injured by it.

Paedagogus

    Our coming here, it seems, then is to no purpose.

Clytemnestra

    Not to no purpose. How can you say "no purpose"?—
    if you have come with certain proofs of death
    of one who from my soul was sprung,
    but severed himself from my breast, from my nurture, who

became an exile and a foreigner;
who when he quitted this land, never saw me again;
who charged me with his father's murder, threatened
terrors against me. Neither night nor day   780
could I find solace in sleep. Time, supervisor,
conducted me to inevitable death.
But now, with this one day I am freed from fear
of her and him. She was the greater evil;
she lived with me, constantly draining
the very blood of life—now perhaps I'll have peace
from her threats. The light of day will come again.

Electra

My God! My God! Now must I mourn indeed
your death, Orestes, when your mother here
pours insults on you, dead. Can this be right?   790

Clytemnestra

Not right for you. But he is right as he is.

Electra

Hear, Nemesis, of the man that lately died!

Clytemnestra

She has heard those she should and done all well.

Electra

Insult us now. For now the luck is yours.

Clytemnestra

Will you not stop this, you and Orestes both?

Electra

We are stopped indeed. We cannot make you stop.

Clytemnestra (to the messenger)

Your coming will be worth much, sir, if you
have stopped my daughter's never ceasing clamor.

Paedagogus (with a feint at departure)

Well, I will go now, if all this is settled.

Clytemnestra

O no! I should do wrong to myself and to   800
the friend who sent you if I let you go.
Please go inside. Leave her out here to wail
the misfortunes of herself and those she loves.

(Clytemnestra and the assumed messenger go into the house.)

Electra

There's an unhappy mother for you! See
how agonized, how bitter, were the tears,
how terribly she sorrowed for her son
that met the death you heard of! No, I tell you,
she parted from us laughing. O my God!
Orestes darling, your death is my death.
By your passing you have torn away from my heart
whatever solitary hope still lingered   810
that you would live and come some day to avenge
your father and my miserable self.
But now where should I turn? I am alone,
having lost both you and my father. Back again
to be a slave among those I hate most
of all the world, my father's murderers!
Is this what is right for me?

                        No, this I will not—
live with them any more. Here, at the gate
I will abandon myself to waste away
this life of mine, unloved. If they're displeased,
let someone kill me, someone that lives within.   820
Death is a favor to me, life an agony.
I have no wish for life.

Chorus

    Where are Zeus's thunderbolts?
    Where is the glowing sun?
    If they see this and hide it
    and hold their peace?

Electra (cries out)
  Oh!

Chorus
  Why do you cry, child?

Electra (cries again)
  Oh!

Chorus
  Speak no great word.   830

Electra
  You will destroy me.

Chorus
  How?

Electra
  If you suggest a hope
  when all is plain, when they are all gone
  to the house of Death, and when I waste
  my life away, you tread me further down.

Chorus
  King Amphiaraus, as I know,
  was caught in woman's golden snares
  and now beneath the earth
  reigns over all the spirits there.

Electra
  Oh! Oh!   840

Chorus
  Alas indeed, for pitiably

Electra
                              he died.

Chorus
  Yes.

Electra
  I know, I know. For him in sorrow
  there came a deliverer.

None such for me. For one there was,
but he is gone, ravished by death.

Chorus

    Unhappy girl, unhappiness is yours!

Electra

I bear you witness with full knowledge.   850
Knowledge too full, bred of a life,
the crowded months surging with horrors
many and dreadful!

Chorus

    We know what you mean.

Electra

So do not then, I pray you,
divert my thoughts to where . . .

Chorus

    What do you mean?

Electra

. . . there is no hope, no kinsfolk,
and none among the nobles that will help.

Chorus

    Death is the common lot of death-born men.   860

Electra

Yes, but to meet it so,
as he did, poor darling,
tangled in the leather reins,
among the wild competing hoofs.

Chorus

    None can guess whence death will come.

Electra

True indeed. He is now a stranger
that was hidden in earth, by no hand of mine,
knew no grave I gave him,
knew no keening from me.   870

(Enter Chrysothemis.)

Chrysothemis
My darling,
I am so glad, I have run here in haste,
regardless of propriety. I bring you
happiness and a relief from all
the troubles you have had and sorrowed for.

Electra
Where could you find a cure—and who are you
to find it—for my troubles which know no cure?

Chrysothemis
We have Orestes here among us—that is
my news for you—as plain as you see myself.

Electra
Are you mad, poor girl, or can it be you laugh
at what are your own troubles as well as mine?   880

Chrysothemis
I swear by our father's hearth. It is not in mockery
I speak. He is here in person with us.

Electra
                    Ah!
Wretched girl! Who told you this that you believed him,
too credulous?

Chrysothemis
                    My own eyes were the evidence
for what I saw, and no one else.

Electra
                    Poor thing!
Poor thing! What proof was there to see? What did you
see that has set your heart incurably
afire?

Chrysothemis
                    I pray you, hear me by the Gods,
and having heard me, call me sane or foolish.   890

Electra

Tell me, then, if the story gives you pleasure.

Chrysothemis

Yes, I will tell you all I saw.
When I came to our father's ancient grave,
I saw that from the very top of the mound
newly spilled rills of milk were flowing. Round
the coffin was a wreath of all the flowers
that grow. I saw in wonder, looked about
for someone who would be near me. When I saw
that all was quiet, I approached the grave.   900
At the top of the pyre there was a lock of hair;
as soon as I saw that, something jumped within me
at the familiar sight. I know I saw
the token of my dearest, loved Orestes.
I took it in my hands, never saying a word
for fear of saying what would be ill-omened,
but with my joy my eyes were filled with tears.
Both then and now I know with certainty
this offering could come from him alone.
Whom else could this concern, save you and me?
I did not do it, I know, and neither did you.   910
How could you? For you cannot leave this house,
even to pray, but they will punish you for it.
Nor can it be our mother. She is not inclined
to do such things, nor, doing them, to be secret.
These offerings at the grave must be Orestes'.
Darling, take heart. It is not always the same
Genius that stands by the same people. Till now
he was hateful to us. But now perhaps
this day will seal the promise of much good.

Electra

Oh, how I have been pitying you for your folly!

Chrysothemis

What is this? Do I not say what is to your liking?   920

Electra

You do not know where you are, nor where your thoughts are.

Chrysothemis

Why should I not have knowledge of what I saw?

Electra

He is dead, my dear. Your rescue at his hands
is dead along with him. Look to him no more.

Chrysothemis

Alas! From whom on earth did you hear this?

Electra

From one that was near to him, when he was dying.

Chrysothemis

Where is he then? I am lost in wonderment.

Electra

In the house. He is our mother's welcome guest.

Chrysothemis

Alas again! But who then would have placed   930
these many offerings on our father's tomb?

Electra

I think perhaps that someone put them there
as a remembrance of the dead Orestes.

Chrysothemis

Unlucky I! I was so happy coming,
hurrying to bring my news to you, not knowing
what misery we were plunged in. Now when I've come,
I find both our old sorrow and the new.

Electra

That is how you see it. But now listen to me,
and you can relieve the suffering that weighs on us.

Chrysothemis

How can I bring the dead to life again?   940

Electra

This is not what I mean. I am no such fool.

Chrysothemis

What do you bid me do, of which I am capable?

Electra

To have the courage to follow my counsel.

Chrysothemis

If I can help at all, I will not refuse.

Electra

Look: there is no success without hardship.

Chrysothemis

I see. As far as my strength goes, I will help.

Electra

Hear me tell you, then, the plans that I have laid.
Friends to stand by and help us we have none—
nowhere—you know that quite as well as I.
Death has taken them and robbed us. We alone,   950
the two of us, are left.
While I still heard my brother flourished,
alive, I had my hopes he would still come,
some day, to avenge the murder of his father.
But now that he's no more, I look to you,
that you should not draw back from helping me,
your true-born sister, kill our father's murderer
that killed him with his own hand—Aegisthus.
There is nothing I should now conceal from you.
What are you waiting for, that you are hesitant?
What hope do you look to, that is still standing?
Now you must sorrow for the loss of fortune   960
that was our father's. Now you must grieve
that you have already so many years
without a marriage and a husband. Do not
hope you will get them now. For Aegisthus
is not such a fool to suffer to grow up
children of you and me, clearly to harm him.
But if you follow my plans,

first, you will win from that dead father, gone
to the underworld, and from our brother with him,
the recognition of your piety.
And, secondly, as you were born to freedom,   970
so in the days to come you will be called free
and find a marriage worthy of you; for all
love to look to the noble.
Do you not see how great a reputation
you will win yourself and me by doing this?
For who of citizens and foreigners
that sees us will not welcome us with praise:
"These are two sisters, friends. Look on them well.
They saved their father's house when their foes
were riding high, stood champions against murder,
sparing not to risk their lives upon the venture.   980
Therefore, we all should love them, all revere them,
and all at feasts and public ceremonies
honor these two girls for their bravery."

This is what everyone will say of us,
in life and death, to our undying fame.
My dear one, hear me. Take sides with your ther
and with your brother. Give me deliverance
from what I suffer. Deliver yourself, knowing this:
life on base terms, for the nobly born, is base.

Chorus
        In such concerns forethought is an ally   990
        to the one that gives, and her that gets advice.

Chrysothemis
        Ladies, before she spoke, if she had good sense,
        she would have held to prudence, as she has not.

                                        (*To Electra.*)

        To what can you look to give you confidence
        to arm yourself and call on me to help?
        Can you not see? You are a woman—no man.

Your physical strength is less than is your enemies'!
Their Genius, day by day, grows luckier
while ours declines and comes to nothingness.   1000
Who is there, plotting to kill such a man
as this Aegisthus, would come off unhurt?
We two are now in trouble. Look to it that
we do not get ourselves trouble still worse
if someone hears what you have said.
There is no gain for us, not the slightest help,
to win a noble reputation if
the way to it lies by dishonorable death.
For death is not the worst but when one wants
to die and cannot even have that death.
I beg of you, before you utterly
destroy us and exterminate our family,   1010
check your temper. All that you have said to me
shall be, for my part, unspoken, unfulfilled.
Be sensible, you, and, at long last, being weaker,
learn to give in to those that have the strength.

Chorus

>Give heed to her. No greater gain for man
>than the possession of a sensible mind!

Electra

>You have said nothing unexpected. Well
>I knew you would reject what I proposed.
>The deed must then be done by my own hand
>alone. For I will not leave it unfulfilled.   1020

Chrysothemis

>Ah!
>I would you had felt so when our father died.
>You would have carried all before you.

Electra

>I was the same in nature, weaker in judgment.

Chrysothemis

>Practice to keep that judgment through your life.

Electra

That is advice which means you will not help me.

Chrysothemis

Yes—for the effort itself implies disaster

Electra

I envy you your "judgment," hate your cowardice.

Chrysothemis

I will be equally patient when you praise me.

Electra

That you will never experience from me.

Chrysothemis

There's a long future to determine that. 1030

Electra

Begone; for there's no help in you for me.

Chrysothemis

There is, but there's no learning it in you.

Electra

Go and tell all this story to your mother.

Chrysothemis

On my side there is no such hatred as that.

Electra

Understand, at least, how you dishonor me.

Chrysothemis

There is no dishonor, only forethought for you.

Electra

Must I then follow *your* conception of justice?

Chrysothemis

You will think it *ours*, when you come to your senses.

Electra

It is terrible to speak well and be wrong.

Chrysothemis

A very proper description of yourself. 1040

Electra

What! Do you not think that I say what I do with justice?

Chrysothemis

There are times when even justice brings harm with it.

Electra

These are laws by which I would not wish to live.

Chrysothemis

If you made your attempt, you would find that I was right.

Electra

Yes, I will make it. You will not frighten me.

Chrysothemis

Are you sure now? You will not think again?

Electra

No enemy is worse than bad advice.

Chrysothemis

You cannot agree with any of what I say?

Electra

I have made my mind up—and not of yesterday.

Chrysothemis

I will go away then. You cannot bring yourself   1050
to find my words right, nor I your disposition.

Electra

Go then. I will never call you back,
not though you long for it. It would be utter
folly to make so hopeless an attempt.

Chrysothemis

Well, if you think that you are right, go on
thinking so. When you are deep in trouble, then
you may agree with what I said.

Chorus

We see above our heads the birds,
true in their wisdom,

caring for the livelihood   1060
of those that gave them life and sustenance.
Why do we not pay our debts so?
By Zeus of the Lightning Bolt,
by Themis, Dweller in Heaven,
not long shall they go unpunished.
O Voice that goes to the dead below,
carry piteous accents,
to the Atridae in the underworld,
and tell of wrongs untouched
by joy of the dance.

Tell them that now their house is sick,   1070
tell them that their two children
fight and struggle, that they cannot
any more live in harmony together.
Electra, betrayed, alone,
is down in the waves of sorrow,
constantly bewailing her father's fate,
like the nightingale lamenting.
She takes no thought of death;
she is ready to leave the light
if only she can kill
the two Furies of her house.
Was there ever one so noble   1080
born of a noble house?

None of the good will choose to live
basely, if so living
they cloud their renown and die nameless.
O my child, my child, even so you
have chosen the common lot of mourning,
have rejected dishonor,
to win at once two reputations
as wise and best of daughters.

I pray that your life may be lifted high   1090

over your foes,
in wealth and power as much as now
you lie beneath their hand.
For I have found you in distress
but winning the highest prize
by piety toward Zeus
for observance of nature's greatest laws.

Orestes (*disguised as a Phocian countryman*)
I wonder, ladies, if we were directed right
and have come to the destination that we sought?

Chorus
What do you seek? And what do you want here?   1100

Orestes
I have asked all the way here where Aegisthus lives.

Chorus
You have arrived and need not blame your guides.

Orestes
Would some one of you be so kind to tell
the household we have come, a welcome company?

Chorus
This lady, nearest you, will bear the message.

Orestes
Then, lady, will you signify within
that certain men of Phocis seek Aegisthus.

Electra
O God, O God, are these the certain proofs
you bring of rumors we had before you came?

Orestes
I do not know about rumor. Old Strophius sent me   1110
here to bring news about Orestes.

Electra
What is it, sir? How fear steals over me!

Orestes

We have the small remains of him in this urn,
this little urn you see us carrying.

Electra

Alas, Alas! This is it indeed, all clear.
Here is my sorrow visible, before me.

Orestes

If you are one that sorrows for Orestes
and his troubles, know this urn contains his body.

Electra

Sir, give it to me, by the Gods. If he
is hidden in this urn—give it into my hands,   1120
that I may keen and cry lament together
for myself and all my race with these ashes here.

Orestes (speaking to his men)

Bring it and give it to her, whoever she is.
It is not in enmity she asks for it.
One of his friends perhaps, or of his blood.

Electra (speaking to the urn)

Oh, all there is for memory of my love,
my most loved in the world, all that is left
of live Orestes, oh, how differently
from how I sent you forth, how differently
from what I hoped, do I receive you home.
Now all I hold is nothingness,
but you were brilliant when I sent you forth.   1130
Would that you had left life before I sent you
abroad to a foreign country, when I stole you
with these two hands, saved you from being murdered.
Then on that very day you would have died,
have lain there and have found your share,
your common portion, of your father's grave.
Now far from home, an exile, on alien soil

without your sister near, you died unhappily.
I did not, to my sorrow, wash you with
the hands that loved you, did not lift you up,
as was my right, a weight of misery, 1140
to the fierce blaze of the pyre. The hands of strangers
gave you due rites, and so you come again,
a tiny weight inclosed in tiny vessel.
Alas for all my nursing of old days,
so constant—all for nothing—which I gave you;
my joy was in the trouble of it. For never
were you your mother's love as much as mine.
None was your nurse but I within that household.
You called me always "sister." Now in one day
all that is gone—for you are dead. All, all
you have snatched with you in your going, like 1150
a hurricane. Our father is dead and gone.
I am dead in you; and you are dead yourself.
Our enemies laugh. Frantic with joy, she grows,
mother, no mother, whom you promised me,
in secret messages so often, you
would come to punish. This, all this, the Genius,
the unlucky Genius of yourself and me,
has stolen away and sent you back to me,
instead of the form I loved, only your dust
and idle shade. Alas! Alas!

(*She takes up an attitude of formalized mourning by the urn.*)
O body pitiable! Alas! 1160
O saddest journey that you went, my love,
and so have ended me! Alas!
O brother, loved one, you have ended me.
Therefore, receive me to your habitation,
nothing to nothing, that with you below
I may dwell from now on. When you were on earth,
I shared all with you equally. Now I claim
in death no less to share a grave with you.
The dead, I see, no longer suffer pain. 1170

Chorus

 Think, Electra, your father was mortal,
 and mortal was Orestes. Do not sorrow too much.
 This is a debt that all of us must pay.

Orestes

 Ah!
 What shall I say? What words can I use, perplexed?
 I am no longer master of my tongue.

Electra

 What ails you? What is the meaning of your words?

Orestes

 Is this the distinguished beauty, Electra?

Electra

           Yes.
 A miserable enough Electra, truly.

Orestes

 Alas for this most lamentable event!

Electra

 Is it for me, sir, you are sorrowing?   1180

Orestes

 Form cruelly and godlessly abused!

Electra

 None other than myself must be the subject
 of your ill-omened words, sir.

Orestes

        O, alas!
 For your life without husband or happiness!

Electra

 Why do you look at me so, sir? Why lament?

Orestes

 How little then I knew of my own sorrows!

Electra

 In what of all that was said did you find this out?

Orestes

So great, so sore, I see your sufferings.

Electra

It's little of my suffering that you see.

Orestes

How can there be things worse than those I see?

Electra

Because I live with those that murdered him.   1190

Orestes

Murderers? And whose? Where is the guilt you hint at?

Electra

My father's murderers. I am their slave perforce.

Orestes

Who is it that forces you to such subjection?

Electra

She is called my mother—but like a mother in nothing.

Orestes

How does she force you? Hardship or violence?

Electra

With violence and hardship and all ills.

Orestes

You have none to help you or to hinder her?

Electra

No. There was one. You have shown me his dust.

Orestes

Poor girl! When I look at you, how I pity you.

Electra

Then you are the only one that ever pitied me.   1200

Orestes

Yes. I alone came here and felt your pain.

Electra

You haven't come as, in some way, our kinsman?

Orestes

I will tell—if (*pointing to the Chorus*) I may speak here among
friends.

Electra

Yes, friends indeed. You may speak quite freely.

Orestes

Give up this urn then, and you shall know all.

Electra

Don't take it from me, stranger—by the Gods!

Orestes

Do what I bid you. You will not be wrong.

Electra

By your beard! Do not rob me of what I love most!

Orestes

I will not let you have it.

Electra

O Orestes!
Alas, if I may not even give you burial!   1210

Orestes

No words of ill omen! You have no right to mourn.

Electra

Have I no right to mourn for my dead brother?

Orestes

You have no right to call him by that name.

Electra

Am I then so dishonored in his sight?

Orestes

No one dishonors you. Mourning is not for you.

Electra

It is—if I hold Orestes' body here.

Orestes

No body of Orestes—except in fiction.

Electra

Where is the poor boy buried then?

Orestes

Nowhere.

There is no grave for living men.

Electra

How, boy,

What do you mean?

Orestes

Nothing that is untrue.   1220

Electra

Is he alive then?

Orestes

Yes, if I am living.

Electra

And are you he?

Orestes

Look at this signet ring
that was our father's, and know if I speak true.

Electra

O happiest light!

Orestes

Happiest I say, too.

Electra

Voice, have you come?

Orestes

Hear it from no other voice.

Electra

Do my arms hold you?

Orestes

Never again to part.

Electra (to the Chorus)
Dearest of women, fellow citizens,
here is Orestes, that was dead in craft,
and now by craft restored to life again.

Chorus
We see, my child, and at your happy fortune   1230
a tear of gladness trickles from our eyes.

Electra
Child of the body that I loved the best,
at last you have come,
you have come, you have found, you have known those you
    yearned for.

Orestes
Yes, I have come.
But bide your time in silence.

Electra
Why?

Orestes
Silence is better, that none inside may hear.

Electra
No, by Artemis, ever virgin.
That I will never stoop to fear—
the women inside there,   1240
always a vain burden on the earth.

Orestes
Yes, but consider that in women too
there lives a warlike spirit. You have proof of it.

Electra
Alas, indeed.
You have awakened my sorrow no cloud can dim,
no expiation wash away,
no forgetfulness overcome,
no measure can fit,
in all its frightfulness.

1250

Orestes

    I know that too. But when you may speak freely,
    then is the time to remember what was done.

Electra

    Every moment, every moment of all time
    would fit justly for my complaints.
    For hardly now are my lips free of restraint.

Orestes

    And I agree. Therefore, hold fast your freedom.

Electra

    By doing what?

Orestes

            Where there is no occasion,
    do not choose to talk too much.

Electra

    Who could find a fit bargain
    of words for that silence,
    now you have appeared?
    Past hope, past calculation,
    I see you.

Orestes

    You see me when the Gods moved me to come.

Electra

    You tell me then of a grace surpassing
    what I knew before, if in very truth
    the Gods have given you to this house.
    This I count an action divine.

Orestes

    Indeed, I hesitate to check your joy;
    only I fear your pleasure may be too great.

Electra

    Orestes, you have come at last,
    have made the journey worth all the world to me,

1260

1270

have come before me at last.
Now that I see you
after so much sorrow,
do not, I beg you—

Orestes
What should I not do?

Electra
                              Do not deprive me
of the joy of seeing your face.

Orestes
I would be angry if I saw another
trying to take me from you.

Electra
                              You agree?

Orestes
                                        Yes.   1280

Electra
My dear one, I have heard you speaking,
the voice I never hoped to hear.
Till now I have held my rage speechless;
I did not cry out when I heard bad news.
But now I have you. You have come,
your darling face before me
that even in suffering I never forgot.

Orestes
Spare me all superfluity of speech.
Tell me not how my mother is villainous,
nor how Aegisthus drains my father's wealth   1290
by luxury or waste. Words about this
will shorten time and opportunity.
But tell me what we need for the present moment,
how openly or hidden we may make
this coming of ours a check for mocking foes.
Take care, you, that our mother may not discover you
by your radiant face, when we two go inside.

Groan as for my destruction, emptily
described in words. For when we have reached success,
then you may freely show your joy, and laugh.   1300

Electra

Brother, your pleasure shall be mine. These joys
I have from you. They are not mine to own.
To grieve you, though it were ever so little,
I would not buy a great good for myself.
If I did so, I would not properly
be servant to the Genius who attends us.
You know the situation. You have heard
Aegisthus is not at home, our mother is.
Do not be afraid that she will see my face
radiant with smiles. Our hatred is too old.   1310
I am too steeped in it. And since I have seen you,
my tears of joy will still run readily.
How can they cease when on the selfsame day
I have seen you dead and then again alive?
For me your coming is a miracle,
so that if my father should come back to life
I would think it no wonder but believe
I saw him. Since your coming is such for me,
lead as you will. Had I been all alone,
I would not have failed to win one of two things,   1320
a good deliverance or a good death for me.

Orestes

Hush, hush! I hear one of the people within
coming out.

Electra (still loudly to the servants of Orestes)

                    In with you, friends and guests,
more so, since what you are carrying in is that
which no one will reject there—nor be glad,
once he has got it.

Paedagogus (coming from inside)

                    Fools and madmen! No
concern for your own lives at all! No sense

to realize that you are not merely near
the deadliest danger, but in its very midst.   1330
If I had not, this while past, stood sentry here
at the door, your plans would now be in the house
before your bodies. I and I only
took the precautions. Have done once and for all
with your long speeches, your insatiate
cries of delight! And in with you at once.
As we are now, delay is ruinous.
It is high time to have done with our task.

Orestes
How shall I find everything inside?

Paedagogus
Well. There is no chance of your recognition.   1340

Orestes
You have announced my death, I understand.

Paedagogus
You are dead and gone—for all your being here.

Orestes
Were they glad of it? Or what did they say?

Paedagogus
I will tell you at the end. As things are now,
all on their side is well—even what is not so.

Electra
Brother, who is this man? I beg you, tell me.

Orestes
Do you not know him?

Electra
                            I cannot even guess.

Orestes
Do you not know him to whose hands you gave me?

Electra
What, this man?

Orestes

               By his hands and by your forethought
I was conveyed away to Phocian country.   1350

Electra

Is this the man, alone among so many,
whom I found loyal when my father was murdered?

Orestes

This is he. There is no need for further questions.

Electra

O light most loved! O only rescuer
of Agamemnon's house, in what a shape
you come again! Are you indeed that other
who saved me and Orestes from many sorrows?
O most loved hands, service of feet most kind!
To think you have stood beside me for so long,
I not to know you, you to give no sign!
You killed me with your words while you had for me
most sweet reality. Bless you, my father,   1360
for in you I think I see my father. Bless you!
Within the selfsame day, of all mankind
I have most hated and loved you most.

Paedagogus

Enough, I think. As for the story
of the happenings in between, there are many days
and nights, as time comes round, to tell you all
clearly, Electra. But as you two stand here
I say to you: now is your chance to act.
Clytemnestra is alone. No man is there.
If you stop now, you will have others to fight   1370
more clever and more numerous than these.

Orestes

Pylades, we have time no longer for lengthy speeches.
We must get inside as quick as ever we can,
only first worshiping the ancestral Gods
whose statues stand beside the forecourt here.

(Exit Orestes.)

Electra (praying to the statue of Apollo)
    Apollo, Lord, give gracious ear to them
    and to me, too, that often made you offerings,
    out of such store as I had, with hand enriching.
    Lycean One, Apollo, now I pray,
    adore, entreat you on my knees, with all   1380
    the resources that I have, be kind to us,
    help us in the fulfilment of our plans
    and prove to all mankind the punishment
    the Gods exact for wickedness.

Chorus
    See how the War God approaches,
    breathing bloody vengeance, invincible.
    They have gone under the rooftree now,
    the pursuers of villainy,
    the hounds that none may escape.
    So that the dream that hung hauntingly   1390
    in my mind shall not lack fulfilment.
    Stealthy, stealthy, into the house,
    he goes, the champion of dead men,
    to his father's palace, rich from of old,
    with his hands on the tool of blood, new-whetted.
    Hermes, the child of Maia, conducts
    the crafty deed to its end, and delays not.

Electra
    Dear ladies, now is the moment that the men
    are finishing their work. Wait in silence.

Chorus
    What do you mean? What are they doing?

Electra

                           She is preparing   1400
    the urn for burial, and they stand beside her.

Chorus
    Why have you hurried out here?

Electra
To watch
That Aegisthus does not come on them unawares.

Clytemnestra (cries from within the house)
House, O house
deserted by friends, full of killers!

Electra
Someone cries out, inside. Do you hear?

Chorus
What I hear is a terror to the ear.
I shudder at it.

Clytemnestra (cries again)
Oh! Oh!
Aegisthus, where are you?

Electra
Again, that cry!

Clytemnestra
My son, my son,
pity your mother!

1410

Electra
You had none for him,
nor for his father that begot him.

Chorus
City,
and miserable generation, now
the day-to-day pursuing fate is dying.

Clytemnestra
Oh! I am struck!

Electra
If you have strength—again!

Clytemnestra
Once more! Oh!

Electra
Would Aegisthus were with you!

Chorus

>The courses are being fulfilled;
>those under the earth are alive;
>men long dead draw from their killers
>blood to answer blood.

1420

>And here they come. The red hand reeks
>with War God's sacrifice. I cannot blame them.

Electra

>Orestes, how have you fared?

Orestes

>   In the house, all
>is well, if well Apollo prophesied.

Electra

>Is the wretch dead?

Orestes

>   You need fear no more
>that your proud mother will dishonor you.

Chorus

>Stop! I can see Aegisthus clearly
>coming this way.

Electra

>Boys, back to the house!

1430

Orestes

>He is in our power!

Electra

>He walks from the suburb full of joy.

Chorus

>Back to the vestibule, quick as you can.
>You have done one part well. Here is the other.

Orestes

>Do not be concerned, we will do it.

Electra

Go

where you will, then.

Orestes

See, I am gone *(hiding himself)*.

Electra

Leave what is here to me.

Chorus

A few words spoken softly in his ear
would be good, that unawares
he may rush to his fight where Justice   1440
will be his adversary.

Aegisthus

Which of you knows where the Phocians are?
I am told they are come here with news for me
that Orestes met his end in a chariot wreck.
You there, yes, I mean you, you, you—
you have been bold enough before, and I should think
it is you these news concern most and therefore
you will know best to tell me.

Electra

I know. Of course. Were it not so, I would
be outcast from what concerns my best beloved.

Aegisthus

Where are the strangers then? Tell me that.   1450

Electra

Inside. They have found their hostess very kind.

Aegisthus

And do they genuinely report his death?

Electra

Better than that. They have brought himself, not news.

Aegisthus

Can I then see the body in plain sight?

Electra

You can indeed. It is an ugly sight.

Aegisthus

What you say delights me—an unusual thing!

Electra

You may delight, if you can find it here.

Aegisthus

Silence now! (*to the servants*) I command you, open the doors
for Mycenaeans, Argives all, to see
that if there be a man whom empty hope   1460
has still puffed up, he may look on the dead
and so accept my bitting, so may shun
a forcible encounter with myself
and punishment to make him grow some sense.

Electra

I have done everything on my side. At long last
I have learned some sense, agreement with the stronger.

Aegisthus (*looking at the shrouded corpse*)

O Zeus, I see an image of what happened
not without envy of Gods. If that is something
I should not say, because of Nemesis,
I take it back. Draw all the covers from
his face that kinship at least may have due mourning.

Orestes

Touch it yourself. This body is not mine,   1470
it is only yours—to see and greet with love.

Aegisthus

True. I accept that. Will you call out
Clytemnestra if she is at home?

Orestes

               She is near you.
You need not look elsewhere.

Aegisthus (as the face of Clytemnestra confronts him)
                              What do I see?

Orestes

Something you fear? Do you not know the face?

Aegisthus

Who are you that have driven us into the net
in which this victim fell?

Orestes

                              Did you take so long
to find that your names are all astray
and those you call the dead are living?

Aegisthus

                              Ah!
I understand. And you who speak to me   1480
can only be Orestes.

Orestes

Were you, so good a prophet, so long misled?

Aegisthus

This is my end then. Let me say one word.

Electra

Not one, not one word more,
I beg you, brother. Do not draw out the talking.
When men are in the middle of trouble, when one
is on the point of death, how can time matter?
Kill him as quickly as you can. And killing
throw him out to find such burial as suit him
out of our sights. This is the only thing
that can bring me redemption from
all my past sufferings.   1490

Orestes (to Aegisthus)

In with you, then. It is not words that now
are the issue, but your life.

Aegisthus
                           Why to the house?
Why do you need the dark if what you do
is fair? Why is your hand not ready to kill me?

Orestes
You are not to give orders. In where you killed him,
my father, so you may die in the same place!

Aegisthus
Must this house, by absolute necessity,
see the evils of the Pelopidae, now and to come?

Orestes
Yours it shall see, at least.
At least yours. There I am an excellent prophet.

Aegisthus
Your father did not have the skill you boast of.   1500

Orestes
Too many words! You are slow to take your road.
Go now.

Aegisthus
               You lead the way.

Orestes
                           No, you go first.

Aegisthus
Afraid that I'll escape you?

Orestes
No, but you shall not
die as you choose. I must take care that death
is bitter for you. Justice shall be taken
directly on all who act above the law—
justice by killing. So we would have less villains.

Chorus
O race of Atreus, how many sufferings
were yours before you came at last so hardly
to freedom, perfected by this day's deed.   1510

IPHIGENIA IN TAURIS

Translated by Witter Bynner

INTRODUCTION

The date of this play is uncertain, but approximately 414 B.C. is a fairly safe guess.

The story involves two important variants on the legend of the House of Atreus: the transportation of Iphigenia to the Tauric Chersonese on the northern coast of the Black Sea; and the last wanderings of Orestes, which unite him with his lost sister. These variants are clearly explained in the text, at lines 1-41 and 940-78, respectively.

Iphigenia in Tauris is technically a tragedy, that is, a serious play in serious poetical language presented in a tragic series and on the occasion when tragedies were produced. But in the modern sense of the term it is not "tragic." It has often been called "romantic comedy," of a type also exemplified in Euripides' *Helen*, his *Ion*, and many lost plays by various Greek dramatists. It is not merely a matter of the happy ending. Other tragedies have that. But here the emphasis is, even more than usually, on plot, on the how rather than the why of the story. Danger hovers, there is excitement, but no catastrophe; the first climax comes in recognition, the second in escape. The plot is excellent indeed, and the mechanism of the recognition scene is one of the best ever contrived. But despite the presence of genuine emotion, chiefly homesickness, something has been lost. One need only compare the "straight" Orestes of this play with the tormented soul in Euripides' own *Electra* or in his *Orestes*.

CHARACTERS

Iphigenia

Pylades

Orestes

Temple Maidens

The Herdsman

Soldiers

King Thoas

Athena

IPHIGENIA IN TAURIS

SCENE: *Out of a temple by the seaside in Tauris, down steps leading to a blood-stained altar seen through its door, comes Iphigenia, the High Priestess, and stands alone on the stairway above the empty court.*

Iphigenia

    Pelops, the son of Tantalus, by maiming
A chariot, won a bride, who bore him Atreus,
And Atreus had two sons, one Menelaus,
The other Agamemnon, who in turn
By Clytemnestra had a child, and I
Am she, Iphigenia.   5
                    People believe
That I was sacrificed by my own father
To Artemis, in the great pursuit of Helen,
Upon an altar near the bay of Aulis,
There where the long deep waves are caught and broken
Hither and thither by the winds, the bay
Where Agamemnon's fleet, his thousand ships   10
From Hellas, waited to avenge on Troy
The wrong done Menelaus through the loss
Of Helen. But a storm came up and still
Another storm and neither sea nor wind   15
Would favor Agamemnon. So he asked
Calchas, the soothsayer, to consult the flame.
And this is what was answered: "Agamemnon,
Captain of Hellas, there can be no way
Of setting your ships free, till the offering
You promised Artemis is given Her.
You had vowed to render Her in sacrifice   20
The loveliest thing each year should bear. You have owed
Long since the loveliness which Clytemnestra
Had borne to you, your daughter, Iphigenia.
Summon your daughter now and keep your word."

They sent Odysseus and his artful tongue
To lure me from my mother by pretending
That I should wed Achilles. When I had come   25
To Aulis, they laid hands on me. The flame
Was lit. The blow would have been struck—I saw
The knife. But Artemis deceived their eyes
With a deer to bleed for me and stole me through
The azure sky. And then She set me down
Here in this town of Tauris, this abode   30
Of savage men ruled by their uncouth king,
Thoas, a horseman headlong as the wind,
Who stationed me High Priestess in Her temple,
And still I serve Her on Her festal days.
Service may seem a holy word. But far   35
From holy are these orders I am bound
To obey, never to question: Her command that I
Must serve to Her the lives of foreigners.
It was a custom long before I came,
An ancient cruel custom. Can She hear me?
My hands prepare the victims. Other hands,
There in the inner temple, spill the blood,   40
Which then is poured upon this altar-stone.

(She descends the steps into the court.)

I dreamed last night a deathly dream. Perhaps
The morning will dispel it if I speak it—
I dreamed that I was far beyond the seas.
I seemed to be at home again in Argos,
Asleep among my maidens—when a roll   45
Of thunder shook the ground. I ran outside.
I watched the house. I saw the coping fall,
The cross-beams stir and yield, break and give way,
Then the whole palace plunge from roof to base,
Only one column left upright in all   50
My father's house. But that one stood alive,
A man with bright brown hair and breathing lips.

And then against my will my hand went out,
As it does toward strangers here condemned to die,
And touched his forehead with this fatal water—
And with water of my tears, because I knew
The dream was of Orestes and his end.   55
The pillar of a family is the son.
This water is the certain sign of death.
It could not mean my family next of kin;
Strophius, my uncle, never had a son.
It was my brother whom I touched with tears—   60
For whom I now must pour a funeral-urn,
All I can do for one so far away.

(Climbing the steps.)

Where are the women from Greece the King appointed
To live with me and help me here in the temple?
I wonder where they are. I need their help.   65

(She enters the temple.)

The voice of Orestes

Keep a sharp lookout. Somebody may be coming.

Pylades

(Entering by the path from the bay.)

I have looked in both directions and there's no one.

Orestes

(Following him and gazing at the temple.)

Is this the shrine of Artemis we have sailed
So many seas to find since we left Argos?
Is it, O Pylades? Is this the shrine?   70

Pylades

I think it is, Orestes. So do you.

Orestes

And might that stone be stained with blood of Greeks?

Pylades

If ever I saw blood—look, on the edge!

Orestes

Look, near the roof! Belongings of the dead!

Pylades

Trophies of foreigners these men have murdered!   75

Orestes

Careful!
            O Phoebus, why must Thy oracle
Bring this on me again, the sight of blood
Again? Have I not seen enough of blood?
My mother shed my father's blood, I hers.
And then the Furies, with their eyes bloody,
Hunted me, hounded me across the land   80
Until at last I ran to Thee and begged
An end of all the cycles of despair
That sped me, hurled me, maddened me through Hellas.
The answer was, "Go to the Taurian country   85
Where Artemis, my sister, has a shrine.
Find there Her statue which had fallen down
From Heaven. Then prove yourself a man able
Enough or fortunate enough to steal it,
Stalwart enough to face all risk and bring it
Home to the holy land of Attica."   90
Although no more was said, I understood
That this would mean the end of my afflictions.
And here I am, O Phoebus, far from home
On a misbegotten shore—doing Thy will.

But Pylades, my fellow venturer,   95
Where can we turn? What man could possibly
Scale these high walls? Or climb the open stairs
And not be seen? Or force the brazen locks
Without whoever is behind them hearing?
If we are caught, it will be certain death,   100
Your death as well as mine. Even this waiting,
Wondering what to do, may cost our lives.
Enough of it! Enough! Back to the ship!

Pylades

    What do we know of flight? How should we dare
    To take a course of which our hearts know nothing?
    Why should we disobey Apollo's order,   105
    Do him dishonor? No, we shall find a way.
    Come, let us leave the temple, let us look
    For a dark cave to hide in. Not the ship!
    By now they must have spied the ship from shore.
    They'd be ahead of us, catch us and end us.   110
      Notice the opening between those beams?
    It's wide enough. Under the night's dim eye
    We could drop through and hoist a wooden statue.
    A coward turns away but a brave man's choice   115
    Is danger. And by all the Gods, shall we,
    Coming this far, now at the end turn back?

Orestes

    I should have been the one to say those words.
    Yes, let us go and find a hiding-place,
    Keep faith with Phoebus and deserve his help.   120
    Have we not youth? Youth, with its fill of strength,
    Turning away from any task should be ashamed.

        (They leave by the path to the shore A great bell rings.
             From the town side the Temple Maidens
                 assemble in the courtyard.)

A Maiden

    Let those who dwell close to these Clashing Rocks
      That guard the Euxine Sea,   125
    Keep silence now before Latona's daughter,
    Artemis, Goddess of the pointed hills!

        (Turning toward the temple as the bell ceases.)

      O Artemis, I come
    On consecrated feet into Thy court,
      I hail Thee beautiful   130
    As the golden gleaming of Thy colonnades!

A Second Maiden

Thy priestess calls us, she who keeps Thy keys,
 Who left behind, for Thee,
Her land of Hellas, the embattled towers,
The shore of horses, and the quiet fields
 Wherein our fathers lived.   135
And we obey her call to worship Thee
 In this embittered land,
Far from Eurotas and from happiness.

  (*Iphigenia enters from the temple, carrying a heavy golden urn.*)

A Third Maiden
    (*Crossing to Iphigenia and taking it to hold for her.*)

O daughter of the king who gathered ships
 A thousand strong and led
Unnumbered men against high-towering Troy,
We heard your call and we have come to you.
 Why have you summoned us?   140
What makes your cheek so thoughtful and so pale?
 What has your tongue to tell,
That your brow is dark and bowed upon your hands?

Iphigenia

My maidens, listen. Listen while I tell
What I have seen. The Muse has veiled Her face,   145
And I am mourning for a dead kinsman.
Last night in a dream I saw my family's ending,
So grieve for me. I saw my brother dead.   150
The dream was clear. My father's house is fallen,
My race broken and gone, Orestes dead!
So grieve for all of us, for all his people.   155
Fate, in still scourging me, takes from all Argos
My only brother!
    To the vanished dead
I shall now pour an offering, a gift   160
Upon the earth, commingled of the milk

Of mountain-kine and of the wine of Bacchus
And of the honey that the russet bees
Gathered, a soothing gift. This and my heart.   165

(*To the Third Maiden.*)

Give me the urn of gold which heavy holds
My tribute to the God of Death.
                              This urn,
Orestes, son of Agamemnon, you   170
Who are lying under the dark earth, I lift
And pour—for you. And may the sweetness reach
And ease your lips. Better I cannot give,
I cannot bring to you braids of my hair
And, crying, lay them down upon your grave.   175
Yet, though from childhood you have thought me dead,
I still can cry—far from my home and you.

A Fourth Maiden

O Lady, woe is in me for your woe,
    My words are like a song
Of old which mourners in the far-off East   180
Chant for the dead, reciting only death,
    A requiem of hell,
A wail of no returning and no hope,
    Using no note of glory,
Only the desolation of the grave.   185

The First Maiden

Mourn for the sons of Atreus, in whose house
    The hearth can never burn.
Mourn for their bitter heritage, a home
Which waits the coming of a happy king   190
    But cannot give him welcome.
Trouble was born forever in their sky
    When Pelops tricked a car
Of toppling horses out of the race for a bride.

The Third Maiden

    Because of a golden lamb which long ago   195
        Beckoned contesting men,
    Mischief began to undermine your house.

The Fourth Maiden

    Vengeance has made its unappeasèd way
        With every dart of death   200
    And visited your family one by one.
        And now with eager hand
    Fate is pursuing you. Your turn has come.

Iphigenia

    Oh bitter my beginning in the womb
    Of her who bore me, from the very night
    When she conceived! Appointed by the Fates   205
    To suffer in this world, I was a child
    Accursed. Yet how she cherished me, her first-born,
    And thrilled that I, of all the girls of Argos,   210
    Should be a bride upon the way to Troy!
        What had she borne me for and loved me for?—
    To be destroyed by my own father's hand,
    To come, behind the horses of delight,   215
    Not to Achilles—but to grief and horror!
        And now beside this melancholy sea
    I live my days—lonely, no love, no friends,
    Wife of no man and mother of no child.   220
    I know no home. I sing no Argive song
    With Argive women to the Queen of Heaven.
    I weave upon the whirring loom no tale
    Of Pallas routing Titans. . . . Oh, instead,
    I face an altar soaked with bloody death.   225
    I hear the cry for pity and the moans
    Of men—a thing too hideous to be told.
        Yet even that seems little to me now—
    Now that a throne is empty and his eyes   230

Are done with weeping, as I wish mine were.
I who have loved him through these lonely years
Shall never see him now but as I left him,
A little baby at his mother's breast—
I who had thought to see him as a king.   235

The Second Maiden

                                        (*Pointing.*)

That herdsman running, stumbling, from the beach!
        What can have happened there?

                                (*They watch the sea-path.*)

A Herdsman

                            (*Entering out of breath.*)

O daughter of the house of Agamemnon,
I bring you news!

Iphigenia

                        Urgent enough for this
Rough outcry in the temple-yard?   240

The Herdsman

                        A ship
From sea has passed through the Symplegades!
And through the fog two fellows waded ashore,
And never was a finer offering
Than these two boys will be for Artemis!
I have been sent to tell you to make ready.   245

Iphigenia

Where are they from?—what country? Could you say?

The Herdsman

From Hellas, but I couldn't say which part.

Iphigenia

What were their names? Perhaps you heard their names?

The Herdsman

One of them called the other Pylades.

Iphigenia

And the one who spoke?

The Herdsman

I didn't hear his name.   250

Iphigenia

Where were they captured?

The Herdsman

Right there on the shore.

Iphigenia

What were you herdsmen doing on the shore?

The Herdsman

Washing our cattle there.

Iphigenia

Tell me again.   255
How were they captured? This is the first time
In all the years I have been living here
That any of you ever brought a Greek
To be the offering. Never a Greek.

The Herdsman

Just as we drove our cattle from the woods   265
To that long hollow where the curving tide
Has cut away the cliff, where the beach-men rest
From purple-fishing, one of us ahead
Came stealing back on tiptoe and he warned us,   265
"Those are not men but Gods! Behind that rock!
Not men but Gods!" And then another herdsman
Caught sight of them, raised up his hands and prayed,
"Palaemon, born of a Sea-Goddess, Master of Ships,   270
Protect us, whether these boys be the Twins
Of Battle, sons and favorites of Zeus,
Or else be brothers of the Ocean Nymphs,
Be sons of Nereus, God of Waves like Thee!"

But another jeered at us and laughed out loud, 275
So that I thought the Gods would turn on him.
But he was sure there must have been a wreck,
And these were sailors looking for our cave
To hide in, having heard that strangers here
Are sacrificed. And he persuaded most 280
Of us, and we were thinking what to do,
When one of them ran out around the rock.
Just staring, not at us or anything
That we could see, but at the air and shook
And groaned, ducking his head from side to side
Behind his arms as if he'd gone insane.
And he was calling out, sharp as a hunter,
"Look, Pylades! O look at her! O look! 285
There! There! Surely you see her now!—that Fiend
From Hell! And on her head look at the snakes,
Their mouths wide open, writhing for my blood!
Here comes another one! And look at that one
Up on the cliff, vomiting fire on me,
Lifting my mother's body like a rock
So she can smash it down on me and kill me! 290
Pylades, help me! They are all around me!"
And we could tell, by the way he jerked his head
Whenever a dog barked or a cow mooed,
That if a Fury wasn't chasing him
He thought there was in every sound he heard.

He might have knocked us flat there in a row, 295
We were so stunned. Instead, drawing his sword,
He lunged into our cattle like a lion,
As if they were the Furies, ripped their sides
With all his might till blood was running down,
Staining the edge. We were just untrained herdsmen 300
Facing expert young swordsmen; but we saw
The cattle wounded and dying and we hunted
For sticks and stones and blew our shells for help
And pretty soon farmers enough had joined us

To fight. Then, as we slowly started forward,   305
His madness left him. I can see him now—
Standing a moment. While I watch he drops
In a heap and foaming at the lips. Once more
We started toward him with our sticks and stones,
But still, his comrade, unafraid of us,   310
Leaned down to wipe the frothy mouth and laid
A piece of linen over the face to shield it—
Till suddenly the fallen man stood up,
Calm and himself again, and faced the rush
Of rocks we heaved at him like breaking waves.   315
We crowded in on him from every side.
He gave one groan as we surrounded him,
Ready to capture him or finish him.
And then we heard his voice ring out and say,   320
"If this is death, let's meet it, Pylades,
Like men! Come on! Together! With our swords!"
   The metal flashed at us. We backed and tricked them
Into the hollow. There, while some of us
Would run for cover, others could throw rocks   325
To draw the swordsmen off and then give way
And let the first lot rally with new armfuls.
And yet we couldn't seem to hit those fellows.
I don't see how it was, with all the stones
We threw at them, that hardly one went straight.
All we could manage was to wear them down   330
By working round each man, aiming our volleys
Just at his sword, which, once he lost his grip,
He was too winded to pick up again.
   And when we took our prisoners to the king,
He told us we should bring them here, and you
Should get them ready for the sacrifice.   335
   Ask Artemis to send us more of them,
More sailor-boys from Greece, send them to Tauris,
And let more men from Hellas pay with blood
After their shouting for your blood at Aulis.

The First Maiden

This is no ordinary man who has come   340
From shores of Hellas to an alien shore
   And battles like a God.

Iphigenia

Go back and bring me the two foreigners.
I shall be waiting for them when you come.

                              (*The Herdsman leaves.*)

   Poor heart of mine, which always hitherto
Has been compassionate, tender toward strangers,   345
And even yesterday felt a quick pang
At thought of Greeks who might be lost in Tauris,
A crushing dream has changed you overnight.
For since Orestes is no more alive,
Now, where my heart was, there is only stone.   350
Strangers who come today, no matter who,
Will find in me a woman beyond tears.
   Unhappiness, O friends, can harden us
Toward other sorrow harsher than our own.
   If but some heaven-sent wind, forcing a ship
Between the Clashing Rocks, might bring me Helen,   355
The Helen whom I hate, and Menelaus,
That I might make of them the sacrifice,
Let a new Aulis expiate the old,
And vent my vengeance! It was Helen's fault
And his, that Greek hands lifted me at Aulis
And led me like a beast where, at the altar,
My father held the sacrificial knife.   360
I live it all again. My fingers, groping,
Go out to him like this and clutch his beard
And cling about his knees. I cry to him:
"It is you yourself, yourself, who brought me here,
You who deceived my maidens and my mother!   365
They sing my marriage-song at home, they fill
The house with happiness, while all the time

Here am I dying at my father's hands!
You led me in your chariot to take
Achilles for my lord, but here is death   370
And the taste of blood, not kisses, on my lips!"
   And I had left my home with my white veil
Drawn down. I had not taken in my arms
My brother—dead this day—nor kissed my sister.
I had saved all my kisses and embraces   375
For the man I was to marry. Even then
My heart was homesick and was faint with hope
That I should soon be back again in Argos.
   And now, O dead Orestes, you, as I,
Forfeit your heritage and lose your home.
   And what does Artemis ask of me here?—   380
She who forbids approach by any man
Whose hand is stained with bloodshed or with touch
Of childbirth or of burial, finds him
Unclean and bans him. She so delicate
In all these ways will yet demand the blood
Of human beings on Her altar-stone!
It cannot be. How could Latona bear   385
To Zeus so cruel a daughter? It is not true.
It is as false as tales of Tantalus
Feeding the Gods a child. O Artemis,
These people, being murderers themselves,
Are charging Thee with their own wickedness.   390
No! I will not believe it of a God!

                          (*She enters the temple.*)

The Second Maiden

  O Clashing Rocks, under whose shadow the dark
    Threat waits, though through this cleft
  Io fled safe, in her disguise as heifer
  Pursued by the sharp stinging of the gadfly,   395
    Fled beyond Europe's land
  And Europe's sea, fled safe but sick at heart,
    Away from home and kin,

Into the alien wilderness of Asia,
What sort of men would leave the holy streams
    Of Dirce, or the reeds   400
Green-growing in Eurotas, to explore
A bitter beach, to dare these ominous rocks
    Where the seas meet in fog,
Where Artemis, among Her colonnades
    Demanding sacrifice,   405
Receives upon her altar human blood?

The Fourth Maiden

Why have they urged the oarsmen of their ship
    To shake the clinging sea
With a great stroke and to accelerate
With rush of rivalry the racing wind?   410
    Was it to sweep the shores
For riches and to vie in bearing home,
    Each to upbuild his house,
The treasures and the trophies of the world?
That glittering hope is immemorial
    And beckons many men   415
To their undoing. Ever insatiate
They sail the sea and look to foreign towns
    To fill their ships with spoil.
But some men never find prosperity,
    For all their voyaging,
While others find it with no voyaging.   420

The Third Maiden

How have they passed the peril of the Rocks
    That Clash and of the coast
Of Phineus heavy with broken waves?   425
I wonder if they sailed across that reach
    Of sea where mariners
Boast to have looked on Ocean's Fifty Daughters
    Under the windowed waves,
Hand in hand dancing, circling round and singing.   430

The Fourth Maiden

    I wonder if their rudder steered them through
        That other reach of sea
    Where the south wind eases and the southwest wind
    Delights a sail and where the isles are white
        With birds that cover them,
    That rise and wheel and then curve back again,
        Where the wings of ocean brood
    And where Achilles races the dark waters.   435

The First Maiden

    My Lady prayed that Fate might hither bring,
        On the way home from Troy,
    The cause of her great misery. Oh, would   440
    That Helen, Helen had been blown ashore,
        That on her fatal head
    For punishment the holy drops might fall
        And that my Lady's knife   445
    Might find in her the fitting sacrifice!

The Second Maiden

    But I have prayed for a deliverer,
        Some mariner from Hellas
    Able to end my grief and set me free.   450
    Ever I go, though only in a dream,
        Back to my father's house.
    And few have greater riches than the joy
        That comes to us in visions,
    In dreams which nobody can take away.   455

The Third Maiden

    Look, there they are! See the two men in chains!
        The herdsman told the truth.
    We must be quiet now for Artemis.

The Second Maiden

    Can hands even from Hellas be so useless   460
        Against this ritual!

The Fourth Maiden

O Artemis, if Tauris in Thy sight
   Win honor by such gift
As never Greece would take, receive this blood!   465

Iphigenia   *(Entering from the temple.)*

Once more I must believe that Artemis
Desires this worship, once again I serve Her.

        (To some of the Soldiers, who bring in the two youths.)

  Loosen their hands. For in the temple court,
As in the temple during consecration,
Chains are unhallowed things.

                (To the Temple Maidens, who obey.)

                 Enter the temple.   470
Prepare the altar for the sacrifice.

          (Turning to the captives, with Soldiers still by them.)

  I wonder who your mother was, your father,
Whether you have a sister who must lose
Her brothers and lament their bravery.
Fate comes and goes, invisible and mute,   475
And never whispers where Her blow shall fall.
None of us ever sees Her in the dark
Or understands Her cruel mysteries.
Tell me, unfortunate men, where are you from—
You who are far from home and yet must go   480
Farther away from home even than this?

Orestes

But who are you, feeling concern for us?
What could we mean to you that you should care
And make it harder for us with your pity?
What good can come from meeting death with tears?
Only a fool, finding that he must meet it,   485
Wishes to talk about it. If a man
Is sorry for himself, he doubles death:
Is first a coward, then a coward's corpse.

So let a man accept his destiny,
No pity and no tears. The sacrifice   490
Is customary here. We knew it was.

Iphigenia
One of your names was told me by a herdsman.
May I know which of you is Pylades?

Orestes
He, if it does you any good to know.

Iphigenia
And from what town in Hellas?   495

Orestes
                              Does it matter?

Iphigenia
Brothers?

Orestes
            We are—in everything but birth.

Iphigenia
What is your name?

Orestes
                        Call me unfortunate.   500

Iphigenia
That would be pity's name for you.

Orestes
                                    Then say
That I am nobody—safe from derision.

Iphigenia
Your name is too important to be told?

Orestes
Come, sacrifice my body, not my name!

Iphigenia
You will not name for me even your town?   505

Orestes

    I am so soon a townsman of no town.

Iphigenia

    Surely it is not much to tell me that.

Orestes

    It is when one can say a town in Argos!

Iphigenia

    Argos? Not Argos? You are not from Argos?

Orestes

    My town, Mycenae, was a lordly place.   510

Iphigenia

    Then what could make you leave it? Were you banished?

Orestes

    In a way banished—banished by myself.

Iphigenia

    How good it is to see a man from Argos!   515

Orestes

    But not to be one in your company!

Iphigenia

    And let me ask about another town.

Orestes

    But why this questioning?

Iphigenia

                What is the news
Of that most talked-of town in the whole world?
What is the news of Troy?

Orestes

                By all the Gods,
I wish that I had never heard its name!

Iphigenia

    But is it true that Troy is overthrown?

Orestes

Its towers lie broken in the dust. 520

Iphigenia

And Helen?

Has Menelaus taken Helen back?

Orestes

Yes, to the sorrow of a noble man.

Iphigenia

She has brought me sorrow too. Where is she now?

Orestes

Gone back with him to Sparta.

Iphigenia

How I hate

The name of Helen! How all Hellas hates it! 525

Orestes

I have my own reason for hating it.

Iphigenia °

The Achaeans are safely home, as I have heard?

Orestes

Some of them are. It would take long to tell.

Iphigenia

But tell me all you can while there is time!

Orestes

Then ask me all you can and I will answer. 530

Iphigenia

The soothsayer, Calchas? Is he back from Troy?

Orestes

Mycenae people say that he is dead.

Iphigenia

Praise Artemis! And is Odysseus dead?

Orestes
Not back nor dead, they say. Still wandering.

Iphigenia
Oh how I hope he never reaches home! 535

Orestes
Why wish him worse than he has borne already?

Iphigenia
What of Achilles?

Orestes
Dead. The marriage planned
At Aulis never happened.

Iphigenia
Those who know
Know well that it was never meant to happen.

Orestes
Knowing so much, are you yourself from Hellas? 540

Iphigenia
I lived in Hellas, many years ago.

Orestes
No wonder you are asking all these questions.

Iphigenia
What of that king they called The Happy King?

Orestes
I know no happy king. Whom do you mean?

Iphigenia
King Agamemnon.

Orestes
What can I say of him? 545
Nothing at all of him. No, do not ask me.

Iphigenia
I beg you by the Gods do me that favor.

Orestes
The news is death—his and another death.

Iphigenia
O Agamemnon! O King Agamemnon!

Orestes
Can you be kin to him, you care so much? 550

Iphigenia
Remembering his love of life, his pride!

Orestes
All of it ended by a woman's hand.

Iphigenia
O miserable woman! Poor, poor king!

Orestes
I pray, I beg you, ask me no more questions.

Iphigenia
Only about his queen. Is she alive? 555

Orestes (doggedly)
His queen is dead. Her own son killed her.

Iphigenia
                          Why?

Orestes
To punish her for murdering his father.

Iphigenia
It was exact of him. I pity him.

Orestes
As well you may, since no God pities him. 560

Iphigenia
Of Agamemnon's children, who is left?

Orestes
Electra—but her husband far from her.

Iphigenia
> The one they sacrificed—what do they say?

Orestes
> Nothing of her, except that she is dead.

Iphigenia
> And he could kill his child—that "happy king!"   565

Orestes
> It was a wicked war for a wicked woman,
> And all the waste that has come from it is wicked.

Iphigenia
> The son of the king? He too is dead in Argos!

Orestes
> Not dead but not in Argos, not in Argos.
>   (*The Temple Maidens return to the court.*)

Iphigenia (telling them)
> I dreamt Orestes dead! It was a lie!

Orestes
> Dreams, lies, lies, dreams—nothing but emptiness!   570
> Even the Gods, with all Their name for wisdom,
> Have only dreams and lies and lose Their course,
> Blinded, confused, and ignorant as we.
> The wisest men follow their own direction
> And listen to no prophet guiding them.
> None but the fools believe in oracles,
> Forsaking their own judgment. Those who know,
> Know that such men can only come to grief.   575

The Second Maiden
> Oh who will bring us news whether our kin
>   Are living or are dead?

Iphigenia
>   (*To Orestes.*)

> For years I have had a plan which now might serve
> As much to your advantage as to mine.

Joint undertakings stand a better chance
When they benefit both sides. So tell me this. 580
Would you, if I could win you leave to do so,
Go back to Argos, with a letter from me
Long ready for a friend of mine who lives there?
My words were written down by one who died
A victim here and yet was sorry for me, 585
Blaming his death on Artemis, not me.
No one had come from Hellas till you came,
No Greek who might be spared and take my letter. 590
But you are gentle, you are the very man
To carry it. You know the names of places
And of persons dear to me. And so I ask
Your help and in return could grant your life,
With one condition—that your friend shall pay 595
The price the state exacts for Artemis.

Orestes

Strange lady, you have made a fair proposal
Save in that one respect. What would my life
Be worth to me, gained by forsaking a friend?
I am the captain of this misadventure
And he the loyal shipmate who stayed by me. 600
A sorry ending if he paid the cost
And I rejected my own enterprise!
Your errand shall be done—but not by me.
Give him your confidence, give him your letter.
To you it makes no difference which of us
Carries your message home. To me it would make
No difference when or how my life should finish
If through continuing it, saving it, 605
I brought disaster on a friend and knew
No honor left in me, no faith, no love.
Besides, this man is dear to me, his life
Is even closer to me than my own.

Iphigenia

Your heart is made of gold. You must have come
From some great seed, to be so true a friend.   610
If only the last member of my line
Be such as you! I have a brother living,
Though face to face with him, I should not know him.
As you have chosen then, so let it be.
Your friend shall take the letter, and you prove   615
Your loyalty by giving him your life.

Orestes

Whose hand is it that brings the touch of death?

Iphigenia

My hand—condemned to it by Artemis.

Orestes

Your hand is still too young a hand for that.

Iphigenia

It is the law.   620

Orestes

            That a woman shall stab men?

Iphigenia

Not that! Oh not the knife! Only the water,
The marking on the forehead—only the water!

Orestes

Whose hand then does the deed, uses the knife?

Iphigenia

Inside the temple—there are men for it.

Orestes

When I am burnt, what happens to my body?   625

Iphigenia

They seal the ashes in a rocky gorge.

Orestes

I wish my sister's hand might tend my body.

Iphigenia

Since she is far away and cannot hear you
Or be with you to give these services,
I shall attend to them. I am from Argos.   630
I will do everything that she might do,
Will bring rich robes to be your final clothing
And funeral ornaments to set about you
And yellow oil to pour, cooling and clean,
Upon the embers. I will melt your ashes
In gold that bees collect from mountain-flowers.   635
You shall be pure and sweet.
                                      While I am gone
To find my letter, do not think ill of me.

                                      (*To the Soldiers.*)

Keep guard, soldiers, without binding these men.

                        (*To herself, pausing as she leaves the court.*)

Oh, if at last my letter should arrive
In Argos and be opened by his own
Beloved hand, a letter never dreamed of,   640
Then he would listen through my opening grave
And hear my living lips cry out to him.

                        (*She leaves, passing around the temple.*)

The First Maiden

O you whose head must feel this water's touch,
     My heart goes out to you!   645

Orestes

Have hope for him, instead of pitying me.

The First Maiden

My heart both pities you and hopes for him
     That he may safely reach
His father's country and be happy there.

Pylades
    Could I desert a friend and still be happy?   650

The First Maiden
    Or I help pitying a man who dies?

The Fourth Maiden
    The one who lives will be the one I pity.

The Third Maiden
        Which is the sadder fate?

The Fourth Maiden
    I cannot tell. I watch and cannot tell   655
    Whether to pity you, or you, the more.
                    (*The Temple Maidens leave the courtyard.*)
Orestes
    What is it, Pylades? What puzzles you?

Pylades
    What do you think it is that puzzles me?

Orestes
    That woman and the way she put her questions.   660
    The sort of questions: the defeat of Troy,
    The Achaeans' homecoming, what happened to Calchas,
    To Achilles, and her being so concerned
    At Agamemnon's death and then inquiring
    About his wife and children. I believe   665
    It true that she herself belongs in Argos
    Or she would never send a letter there
    And care about occurrences in Argos
    As if they flowed within her very veins.

Pylades
    Yes, that is what at first had puzzled me,
    And then I thought it natural enough   670
    That in a place even half civilized
    People should care about the fate of kings.
    But that was not what puzzled me, not that.

Orestes

If we put our heads together, we could surely—

Pylades

How can you wrong me, thinking I would live
And leave you here to die? I came with you.   675
I shall continue with you to the end,
Or I could never show my face again
On an Argive hill or in a Phocian valley
But to be pointed out and rightly spurned
As one who had betrayed a friend. People
Might say worse things than that, the worst   680
An evil mind could think of to enjoy:
That I had wished or even caused your death
To benefit, as husband of your sister,
By my inheritance—to win your throne.
Such thoughts are frightening, but worse my shame
In your imagining that I might leave you.
If you meet knife and flame, then so do I.   685
I am your friend and there's no more to say.

Orestes

How can you be my friend and yet refuse me?
The load I bear can never be laid down—
And would you add to it by lightening yours?
All the contempt you imagine from men's hearts
And tongues, falling on you, would fall on me
In my own heart from my own conduct, if I let   690
The service you have done me bring you harm.
What has Fate left me of my life to cherish
But a good ending? As for you, my comrade,
You have not any right to choose to die.
You have the blessing of your fortunate blood
To make you wish to live. I can but pray
That, by your living, solace may be brought   695
To my ill-fated family. Pylades,
Once home again and with your wife, my sister,

Give me my happiness by having a son
In whom my name shall live, and through your children
Build up once more the house of Agamemnon.
Go back, I say, and make my home your home.
You will be there in Hellas, on the shore
Where Argive horsemen ride. Give me your hand   700
And swear to me that you will build my tomb,
Will set memorials in it and will ask
My sister for a lock of her long hair
To lay with them. Tell her that I was led
Before this altar by a gentle hand,
A woman's hand, a woman born in Argos,   705
And how at last my blood was purified.
   O Pylades, be gentle to my sister!
And so goodbye, my best and closest friend.
When we were boys, we loved sharing our sports.
You rode the hills with me And now in manhood
You are the one who has shared the heartache with me   710
When treacherous Phoebus through his oracle
First lied to me, then tricked me, luring me far
From home, lest watchful eyes in Hellas see
That Gods as well as men break promises.
I trusted Him, with all my faith and will,
Even, at His command, killing my mother,
And in return He has forsaken me.   715

Pylades

I shall obey your will, though not my own;
Shall build your tomb in Hellas. Your heart knows
That I shall love your sister all my life.
And, close to you in your life, my heart knows
That it shall hold you closer in your death—
If death it be. Gods, in mysterious ways,   720
Never explaining, mask the face of life,
Behind what looks like death, disguising life,
And then revealing it.

Orestes

> The time is gone
> When Gods might show that face. For she has come.

Iphigenia

> (*Returning to the temple by the town-path and
> addressing the Attendants who follow her.*)
>
> Precede me into the temple and be ready. 725
>
> > (*The Attendants enter the temple.*)
>
> Here is my letter, safe within these folds.
> But I have wondered. A man who has been in danger
> When he comes out of it forgets his fears,
> And sometimes he forgets his promises. 730
> Might it not happen that your friend, intent
> Upon his own concerns again, forget
> How very much this letter means to me?

Orestes

> And what would you suggest, to ease your mind?

Iphigenia

> His solemn vow to take this where I say. 735

Orestes

> And will you make a vow balancing his?

Iphigenia

> To do what, or undo what?

Orestes

> > To make sure
> He be allowed to leave this deathly place.

Iphigenia

> How could he keep his vow, unless he leave? 740

Orestes

> What makes you think the king will let him sail?

Iphigenia
I can persuade the king and will myself
Go to the ship and see your friend aboard.

Orestes
Then word the vow as you would have him make it.

Iphigenia
You promise the delivery of my letter?

Pylades
I promise the delivery of your letter.   745

Iphigenia
I promise you the king will let you leave.

Pylades
In whose name do you swear?

Iphigenia
                              By Artemis,
Here in Her Temple—and implore Her help.

Pylades
And I by Zeus Himself, by Heaven's King.

Iphigenia
And what if you should fail to keep your word?   750

Pylades
Then may I never again set eyes on Argos.
And what if you should fail in keeping yours?

Iphigenia
Then may I never again set foot in Argos.

Pylades
But we forget one possibility.

Iphigenia
Which might affect the keeping of your vow?

Pylades

> How could I keep my vow if this should happen—   755
> If we were wrecked by a storm, torn by a reef,
> If we were sunk and everything went down,
> And if my life were saved but not the letter.
> If that should happen, how could I keep my word?

Iphigenia

> In any plan, two ways improve on one.
> So I will tell you, slowly, line by line,   760
> The contents of my letter, which, if need be,
> You are to tell my friend. Then he will know.
> For either you will place it in his hand
> And the written words will speak to him or else,
> If they are lost, your voice will be their echo.   765

Pylades

> That is a surer way, for both of us.
> So whom am I to find for you in Argos?
> What shall I say to him?

Iphigenia

>   Say this to him.
> Say to Orestes, son of Agamemnon,
> "A greeting comes from one you think is dead."   770
> Tell him, "Your sister is not dead at Aulis
> But is alive."

Orestes

>   Alive? Iphigenia?
> Oh, no! Unless the dead come back again!

Iphigenia

> You are looking at her now, for I am she.
> But let me finish what I ask of him.
> "O brother, come and save me from a life
> As priestess in a loathsome ritual—   775
> Save me from dying in this lonely land."

Orestes

Where am I, Pylades? What am I hearing?

Iphigenia

"Lest memory of me should always haunt you."
The name, you must repeat it, is Orestes.

Orestes

I hear a God!

Iphigenia

You hear only a woman.

Orestes

I hear a woman—and I hear a God!   780
Let me hear more! I hear a miracle!

Iphigenia

Then tell him, "Artemis put out Her hand
And spared my life at Aulis, leaving a deer
To bleed instead." And tell him this, "My father,
Not looking when he struck, believed me dead.   785
Artemis brought me here." The letter ends.

Pylades

No word was ever easier to keep!
Lady, keep yours or not, I keep mine now!   790
I give you this, Orestes, from your sister!
                                        (*Enter the Temple Maidens.*)

Orestes

How can I look at letters! Let me look—
Oh let me stare at you whom I had lost!
Oh let me touch you with my hands and prove   795
That you are real and hold you close, close!

The Third Maiden

Do not lay hands, whoever you may be,
        Upon a vestment sacred
To Artemis! Do not profane that robe!

« 147 »

Orestes

You are my sister, you are my father's daughter,   800
And nature will not let you turn away
From your own brother given back to you.

Iphigenia

Ah, you would have me think that you are he.
Orestes is not here. He is in Argos.

Orestes

Poor sister, not in Argos! I am here!   805

Iphigenia

You mean Tyndareus was your mother's father?

Orestes

Yes, and my father's grandfather was Pelops.

Iphigenia

What are you saying? How can I believe you?

Orestes

By asking me more questions—about home.

Iphigenia

Say anything—say anything at all.   810

Orestes

Electra used to tell us about Atreus,
About Thyestes, how they came to quarrel.

Iphigenia

The fight they had over the golden lamb!

Orestes

The tapestry you made of it, yourself.

Iphigenia

Are you Orestes? Is it really you?   815

Orestes

Another tapestry you made, of Helios
Changing His course. Have you forgotten that?

Iphigenia

I can remember every single thread.

Orestes

And the bath perfumes, a present for your wedding,
Sent by your mother to Aulis—you remember?

Iphigenia

I live each bitter moment of that day.

Orestes

The lock of hair you sent back to your mother?

Iphigenia

I meant it for my own memorial   820
To mark a grave where I could never lie.

Orestes

The keepsake in your room! Do you remember
The ancient spear, the one Pelops had used
On Oenomaus, when he won from him
Hippodamia as a bride from Pisa?   825

Iphigenia

It is, it is! Orestes! O my brother!
My home has come to me from far away,
For you have come, I have you in my arms.   830

Orestes

And I have you in mine, whom I thought dead.
No wonder that our eyes are blind with tears,
Of joy, not sorrow—yet of sorrow too.

Iphigenia

You were a baby when I sailed away,
Lifted to watch me, held up by your nurse   835
To wave goodbye. And now those little arms
I saw reach out have come to me, grown strong
To comfort me! How can I tell my joy?
There is no language sweet enough to tell it.
There is no joy like this. There never was.   840

Orestes

And there must never be an end of it.

Iphigenia

I am bewildered. And I cannot think
What I should say, my friends. I cannot think
Of anything but joy—except a fear
That he might vanish as he came. O Argos!
My heart is full of my beloved Argos,   845
Of everybody who belongs to Argos,
And of my brother born and bred in Argos
To be a living light honoring Argos!

Orestes

How could the happiness we both were born for   850
Become unhappiness?

Iphigenia

                    Unhappiness
Began for me when my unhappy father
Lifted a knife and drew it toward my throat.

Orestes

I was not there, and yet how plain I see you!

Iphigenia

And do you see what I remember there?   855
The treachery, the misery, the shame!
After the trickery, the vanishing
Of all my dreams! Not to Achilles' arms
I went, circled with songs, but, shaken with sobs,
I felt the hot flame from the altar-stone   860
And the cold water trickled on my head.

Orestes

O desolate daughter of a desolate father!
I see his face. I see his haunted face!

Iphigenia

But why feel pity for the pitiless man
Who caused all this?   865

Orestes

And might have caused today
Your leading your own brother to the grave.

Iphigenia

Some God prevented. But I came so near,
My hand so nearly set the final seal,
That I still shake as though you lay here dead.
We have seen the beginning of a miracle.   870
We found each other and my hand was spared
From signalling your death. How can we now
Fulfill the miracle, make it complete?
How can I save you from some other hand
And speed you safely homeward from this place?   875
There will be many hands, and many swords,
For you to face. How could you match them all?
A giant's task, too much for any man!
There are no weapons possible but wits,
And yet I see you stand there dazed as I.   880
Could you outrun them when they follow you,
Escape them on an inland wooded trail?
Or would a dash through breakers be the way?
Would you be safer trusting to the trail
Or to the ship? Oh, I can see you losing   885
Your way on land, risking a thousand deaths.
The countryside is full of savage men.
The ship is better, even that sharp cleft
Between the Clashing Rocks. Yes, risk the sea.   890
You challenged it, came through it. Having once
Met it and mastered it, you can again.
And so let fly your oars. Yes, risk the sea,
Take to the ship—though who can surely tell
If God or man shall steer you through the waves   895
To a safe landing, or if Fate shall grant
Argos the benison of your return?
Or me—who knows?—the sweet surprise of mine!

The Third Maiden

 I have heard marvelous tales from story-tellers,   900
   But nothing to compare
 With this event which my own eyes have seen.

Pylades

 Orestes, it was natural and right
 For you and for your sister to compare
 Old memories, but surely it's high time
 We think of nothing else but our escape   905
 From this grim place and how to manage it.
 No man, when Fortune beckons him, should wait
 A single instant. He should follow her.

Orestes

 Meet her halfway, you mean, more than halfway,   910
 Since every God helps him who helps himself.

Iphigenia

 But first—I cannot wait—I have to hear!
 Oh tell me just a word about my sister—
 About Electra! Tell me about Electra!

Orestes

 This is the husband who has made her happy.   915

Iphigenia
 This man? But who. . . .

Orestes

       A Phocian. Strophius' son.

Iphigenia
 Then he is Atreus' grandson! He's our kinsman!

Orestes
 Your cousin—my one friend.

Iphigenia

       Not even born
 When I left home to die.   920

Orestes
> > > > He is the son
> > Of Strophius in old age.

Iphigenia
> > > > > I welcome you,
> > My sister's husband.

Orestes
> > > > > And my more than brother.

Iphigenia
> > But oh our mother? You have not said why—

Orestes
> > I said enough—I said she killed our father. 925

Iphigenia
> > You have not told me why.

Orestes
> > > > > > Then do not ask me.

Iphigenia
> > May I not ask if you are king of Argos?

Orestes
> > Not king but exile. Menelaus is king.

Iphigenia
> > When you most needed him, he drove you out? 930

Orestes
> > Not he. The Furies—the avenging Fiends.

Iphigenia
> > Your madness on the beach—it was the Fiends?

Orestes
> > Anyone seeing me might think it madness.

Iphigenia
> > Still chasing you because you killed our mother?

Orestes

They try to choke me with my mother's blood!   935

Iphigenia

What brought you here?

Orestes

Phoebus—His oracle.

Iphigenia

Why should He choose this place?

Orestes

Oh let me tell
My bitter narrative from end to end.
 After my hand had unforgivably   940
Punished my mother's unforgivable sin,
Down on my head they came, the Avenging Furies,
The nameless Fiends. Then Phoebus ordered me
To Athens that I might explain to Them
In the Tribunal Zeus had sanctified   945
To Ares when she answered ancient charges.
 When I arrived there, none of all my friends
Received me. They avoided me at first
As one unclean. Later they pitied me
And gave me food in the same room with them
But at a separate table where they let   950
My meals be served when theirs were, sent me a cup
When their love-bowl was passed, but then would turn
Away and would not look at me nor speak
To me—because I was a murderer. . . .
I tried to act as though I did not care,   955
But sad and lonely when I thought of her
Whom I had killed, I drank a bitter cup.
 I am told Athenians commemorate
My trial with a Service of the Pitcher,
Everyone drinking his own cup in silence. . . .   960
 While I was facing judgment on that hill,

I on one flagging and across from me
The eldest of the Avengers charging me
With murder, Phoebus rose to my defense.
It was His eloquence that saved my life,   965
Persuading Pallas, in the chair, with votes
Cast evenly for and against me, that she add
Her own vote for me—which acquitted me.

　Some of the Fiends, persuaded, went to found
A cellar temple under the Tribunal.
Others denounced the verdict as unfair   970
And flew at me in such a vicious frenzy
That I ran back for help again from Phoebus,
Faint with despair fell down upon my knees
And swore to starve myself to death unless
The God who had ruined me would rescue me.   975

　Out pealed His voice over the golden tripod,
Bidding me find among the Taurians
Their Artemis of wood carven in Heaven
But fallen on their coast and, stealing it,
Establish it for Grecian worshippers
In Attica.

　　　　Help me to do this thing
And to fulfil His mission. Help me, sister!
Once I have carried home in these two hands   980
The image of the Goddess, I am rid
Of madness! And I urge you with a gift
Of rugged rowers rowing you home to Argos!
O my own sister, for our family's sake,
Help me to save that family and ourselves!
Unless you help me take the image back,   985
This very day our family's name shall die.

The Fourth Maiden

Some God is visiting ancestral sin
　　On the house of Tantalus.

Iphigenia

How I had dreamed, long, long before your coming,
Of you and of my country! How my prayer   990
Joins yours for the renewal of our breed—
Even of his whose hand reached for my blood!
Now that no blood of yours stains my own hand,
I have no anger left, but only hope
That in your life the family name shall live.   995
   But if you leave me, taking Artemis,
When the king sees the empty pedestal,
What can I say? How can my life be saved
Unless, with one quick stroke seizing the image,
We flee together to your leaping deck?   1000
If we succeed, what happiness for me!
But even if I fail, you need not fail.
My life is little. I would gladly die
To earn your safety and your reaching home.
If a man die, a house, a name, is lost.   1005
But if a woman die, what does it matter?

Orestes

It mattered when my mother died! If now
You also were to die because of me—!
Whatever happen, we shall share one fate,
Alive in Greece, or here together dead.   1010
   But by all signs, the Gods are on our side.
If Artemis were not, why should it be
Her Brother's oracle commanding me
To bring Her image back? She wishes it!
Here in Her Temple, in Her very presence,
Has come the omen of my finding you!   1015
Yes, we are being guided by the Gods!

Iphigenia

The king will kill us if we steal the statue.

Orestes

Then why not kill the king?   1020

Iphigenia
Anger the Gods
Again? He has been kind to me.

Orestes
Why not,
To save our lives, take chances with the Gods?

Iphigenia
I like your boldness. But it cannot be.

Orestes
What if you hid me somewhere in the temple?

Iphigenia
To steal out after dark?   1025

Orestes
Since I must steal,
The day for honest men, the night for thieves.

Iphigenia
Guards are on watch inside.

Orestes
How else are we—

Iphigenia
We might—

Orestes
Might what?   1030

Iphigenia
Make use of your misfortune.

Orestes
Women have ways of changing ill to good.

Iphigenia
I shall denounce you as a matricide.

Orestes
Make use of any good you find in that.

Iphigenia
    As one unworthy to be sacrificed.   1035

Orestes
    I understand—but not how it would serve us.

Iphigenia
    You are unclean—cannot be purified—

Orestes
    What will that do for us?

Iphigenia
                    except by deep
    Sea-water, beyond stain, off from the shore.

Orestes
    Yes, but our mission, you forget the statue—   1040
    The reason for our coming here.

Iphigenia
                    She too,
    Having been soiled by your approach, must be
    Washed clean, the image too!

Orestes
                I see it now.
    The inlet where the ship—

Iphigenia
               strains at the leash.

Orestes
    And you will bring the image there yourself!

Iphigenia
    Nobody ever touches it but me.   1045

Orestes
    But Pylades? Is he a murderer too?

Iphigenia
    He aided you. He also must be cleansed.

Orestes

    A story for the guards—but for the king?

Iphigenia

    In any case I could not keep it from him.
    So he shall hear it and shall be persuaded.

Orestes

    Fifty stout oars are waiting for the word.   1050

Iphigenia

    That is the part of it I leave to you.

Orestes

    I have but one suggestion. Do these women
    Realize how much their loyalty might mean?
    Women know women. Make your plea to them.
    And after that we are in the hands of Heaven.   1055

Iphigenia

    O friends who have been near and dear to me,
    It may depend upon your carefulness
    Whether or not I reach my home and kin.
    A woman knows how much her weakness needs
    The sympathy and help of other women,   1060
    Their understanding and their loyalty.
    I ask you only this, that you say nothing
    Of what has happened here, that you keep silent.
    The stillest tongue can be the truest friend.
    We three must take a hair's-breadth chance between   1065
    Capture and death, deliverance and home.
    But if we do escape, then we shall work
    For your deliverance, for you and you
    To share our happiness at home in Hellas
    And you and you. Holding your hand, I ask you—   1070
    Kissing your cheek. Clasping your knees, I ask you—
    And you I ask by love of your two parents.

                           (To the Second Maiden.)

And you by love of the child you left behind.
Who will say yes to me? Who could say no
When it might cost my brother's life and mine?

The First Maiden
Rely on me, dear Lady.

The Second Maiden
                    And on me.   1075

The Third Maiden
We shall do everything we can to help.

The Fourth Maiden
By Zeus we pledge silence and loyalty.

Iphigenia
May Heaven reward the hearts behind those words!
                              (*To Orestes and Pylades.*)
Now for your part—and yours—inside the temple.
The king will soon arrive and will be asking   1080
Whether the strangers have been sacrificed.
                    (*Orestes and Pylades enter the temple.*)
O gallant Goddess, having saved me once
At Aulis from my father's deadly hand,
Save with me now my brother and his friend,
Lest Phoebus be disproved because of Thee
And men forsake His oracle. O come   1085
In gracious might away from this bleak place,
Away from gloom, to the lovely light of Athens.
                              (*She follows into the temple.*)

The First Maiden
O sad-voiced ocean-bird, heard in the foam
      Low by the rocky ledge   1090
Singing a note unhappy hearts can hear,
The song of separation from your mate,
      The moan of separation,

I have no wings to seek like you, but I
    Can sing a song like you,   1095
A song of separation from my mate.

The Second Maiden

  At home in Hellas now my kinsmen gather
      Where Artemis is due
  To bless the new-born from her Cynthian hill
  And soothe the mothers with the cooling palm
      And bay and olive-tree,   1100
  Where once Latona loved the winding streams
      And watched the rounded pools
  White with the song-like motion of the swans.   1105

The Third Maiden

  Alas, the falling tears, the towers fallen,
      The taking of our towns!
  Alas, the clang of bright and angry spears
  Which drove me, captive, to an alien ship,   1110
      Whence I was sold away
  To be an exile here, a handmaiden
      With Agamemnon's daughter,
  Doomed to the bloody rites of Artemis!   1115

The Fourth Maiden

  And at this altar where the sacrifice
      Is not of sheep but men,
  I envy those unhappy from their birth,
  For to be bred and seasoned in misfortune
      Is to be iron to it,
  But there is something in the pang of change   1120
      More than the heart can bear,
  Unhappiness remembering happiness.

The Second Maiden

  Lady, a ship is here to take you home,
      And in the rowers' ears
  Pan shall be sounding all his pointed notes,   1125

Great mountains echoing to His little reed,
    And Phoebus on His lyre
Shall strike profound the seven strings and sing
    To you of Attica,   1130
Shall sing to you of home and lead you there.
Oar after oar shall dip and carry you,
    Lady, away from us,
Oar after oar shall push the empty waves
Wider, wider, leaving us lonely here,
    Leaving us here without you,
And forward over the unceasing bow
    The sail shall faster run,   1135
Ever refilling with the unspent wind.

The First Maiden

Oh to fly swifter than the wingèd sun
    Upon his dazzling track!—
And not to let my golden light be folded   1140
Until I touch my house, my roof, my room,
    From which I used to go
To noble marriages and take my place
    In the bright company,
Give them my hands and circle round and dance   1145
And always try to be the loveliest,
    Under my mother's gaze,
In my unrivalled radiance of attire
And in the motion of my hands and feet,
    While my embroidered veil
I would hold closely round me as I danced
    And bowed and hid my cheek   1150
Under the shadow of my clustering curls.

                    (*Enter King Thoas with Soldiers.*)

Thoas

Where is my guardian of the temple gate,
My Grecian girl? Where are the foreigners?
Am I too late to see the sacrifice?
Are the victims' bodies being burnt already?   1155

The Fourth Maiden

    She is coming out herself and she will tell you.

                    (Iphigenia appears in the temple-door, carrying
                              the wooden Artemis.)

Thoas

                              (Starting up the stairs.)

    What does this mean, daughter of Agamemnon?
    Why have you moved the Goddess from her place?

Iphigenia

    O King, stand back—stay back beyond the threshold!

Thoas

    But what has happened that would call for this?   1160

Iphigenia

    Back from contamination! I am abrupt.

Thoas

    Speak bluntly to me. What?

Iphigenia

                   The offerings
    You sent us for the Goddess are impure.

Thoas

    How do you know? What makes you think—

Iphigenia

                      She turned
    Away from them. She moved when they came near.   1165

Thoas

    Mightn't it be a little bit of earthquake
    That moved Her?

Iphigenia

            No. She moved of Her own will
    And even for a moment shut Her eyes.

Thoas

Because their hands were blood-stained? Was it that?

Iphigenia

It was Her divination of their guilt.

Thoas

You mean they'd killed a Taurian on the beach?   1170

Iphigenia

Their guilt was with them when they came—the crime
Of killing their own kin.

Thoas

What kin?

Iphigenia

Mother
Of one of them—a murder they had planned.

Thoas

O great Apollo, what barbarian
Would do the thing these Greeks have done!

Iphigenia

Greeks once
But now disowned by Greeks, driven from Hellas.   1175

Thoas

Even so, why bring the Goddess out?

Iphigenia

Defiled,
She must be purified, be cleaned again
By the touch of Her own sky.

Thoas

How could you know
What sort of crime these fellows had committed?

Iphigenia

I saw Her turn from them. I asked them why.

Thoas
  You are a Greek, quick-witted, a true Greek.   1180

Iphigenia
  They are Greek too, tried to propitiate me
  With welcome news.

Thoas
           Of Argos?

Iphigenia
                Of my brother,
  News of Orestes.

Thoas
          Thought they could weaken you.

Iphigenia
  News that my father is alive and prospers.   1185

Thoas
  But you were firm. You didn't let your feelings—

Iphigenia
  What should I feel toward any Greek but hate?

Thoas
  How shall we deal with them?

Iphigenia
              By temple rules.

Thoas
  Something besides the pitcher and the knife?   1190

Iphigenia
  Complete immersion, for a sin like theirs.

Thoas
  In the bubbling spring? Or is salt water best?

Iphigenia
  The sea is the absorbent of all evil.

Thoas

Artemis says the sea?

Iphigenia

     I say the sea.   1195

Thoas

Breakers are handy—just beyond the wall.

Iphigenia

But these especial rites are secret rites.

Thoas

Then choose your place; no one shall trespass on you.

Iphigenia

And I shall have to wash the Goddess too.

Thoas

Can a Goddess be defiled, the same as people?   1200

Iphigenia

Why did I have to bring Her from the temple?

Thoas

You are a pious woman and I thank you.

Iphigenia

Then will you issue orders for me?

Thoas

         Name them.

Iphigenia

First have the strangers bound with rope.

Thoas

         But why?

Where could they go?

Iphigenia

      O King, beware of Greeks!

Thoas

           (*To his Soldiers.*)

 Bind them.   1205

Iphigenia

   And have them brought to me.

Thoas

         And bring them.

Iphigenia

 But cover both their heads with heavy cloth.

Thoas

 To keep even the Sun from seeing them?

Iphigenia

 Send soldiers with me.

Thoas

      Take your pick of them.

Iphigenia

 And have a herald tell all Taurians—

Thoas

 To what?

Iphigenia

   To stay indoors till this is done.   1210

Thoas

 One step outdoors and they would be polluted.

Iphigenia

 By matricide!

Thoas

           (*To Attendants.*)

   Go tell the herald this.

Iphigenia

 Indoors they stay.

Thoas
My people do concern you!

Iphigenia
The one I am most concerned about—

Thoas
Who? Me?

Iphigenia
Has helpful work to do, inside the temple.   1215

Thoas
To—?

Iphigenia
Purify it with pine smoke from torches.

Thoas
The temple shall be sweet for your return.

Iphigenia
When they come out—

Thoas
What shall I do?

Iphigenia
Hold up
Your sleeve and shield your face.

Thoas
From the contagion.

Iphigenia
And if I seem delayed—

Thoas
How shall I tell?

Iphigenia
Feel no surprise, be patient.

Thoas

You must do,
Carefully, everything the Goddess wants.   1220

Iphigenia

I trust that I can serve Her wish.

Thoas

And mine.
(*The temple doors open for an emerging procession.*)

Iphigenia

And here they come, the strangers in their robes,
And lambs whose blood is used instead of theirs,
And burning torches and the instruments
Needed for purifying them and Her.   1225
   Taurians, turn away from the pollution.
Gate-tenders, open the gates, then wash your hands.
Men who want wives, women who want children,
Avoid contagion, keep away, away!

(*Holding the image high.*)

   O Virgin Goddess, if the waves can wash   1230
And purge the taint from these two murderers
And wash from Thee the tarnishing of blood,
Thy dwelling shall be clean and we be blest! . . .
To Thee and the All-Wise my silent prayer.

(*She signals. The procession moves down the stairs. Carrying
the image, she leads the Soldiers and victims from the foot
of the stairs across the court and out toward the sea.
Thoas enters the temple with Attendants, leaving
in the courtyard only the Temple Maidens.*)

The Second Maiden

Latona bore one day a golden Child,
   Brother of Artemis,   1235
Phoebus, the darling of the vales of Delos—

The First Maiden
　Whose little fingers hovered on the harp
　　And pulled at archery.

The Second Maiden
　Up from His birthplace, to Parnassus' top
　　The Mother brought Her Boy—　　　　　　　　　　1240

The First Maiden
　Where Dionysus vaults the waterfall.

The Third Maiden
　There, hidden coiling in the leafy laurels,
　　A serpent with bright scales　　　　　　　　　　1245
　And blood-red eyes, a creature born of Earth,
　Guarded the cave that held Earth's oracle.
　　Phoebus, beholding it, leaped up
　Out of His Mother's arms, a little Child,　　　　　　1250
　　And struck the serpent dead—

The Second Maiden
　And on that day began His prophecies.

The Fourth Maiden
　O Phoebus, having won the golden throne
　　And tripod of the truth,
　Out of the very center of the Earth,
　Thou couldst hear wisdom; and Thy voice conveyed,
　　Accompanied by all　　　　　　　　　　　　　　1255
　The run and ripple of Castalian springs,
　　The deepest prophecies
　That ever Earth heard whispered out of Heaven.

The Third Maiden
　But Earth had wished to save the oracle
　　For Themis, Her own daughter,　　　　　　　　1260
　And so in anger bred a band of dreams
　Which in the night should be oracular
　　To men, foretelling truth.　　　　　　　　　　1265

And this impaired the dignity of Phoebus
    And of His prophecies.

The Second Maiden

And the baby God went hurrying to Zeus,   1270
Coaxed with His little hands and begged of Zeus
    To send the dreams away.

The First Maiden

And Zeus was very pleased to have His Son
Come straight to Him with troubles. His great brow   1275
    Decided with a nod
That Phoebus have his prize restored to Him,
    In spite of angry Earth,
His throne, His listening throng, His golden voice . . .

The Fourth Maiden

That throats of night be stricken straightway mute   1280
    And plague mankind no more,
That shapes of night no longer hold their power
To foretell truth in syllables of gloom
    And haunt men's aching hearts—
That men be freed from the prophetic dark
    And every shrouded form
And listen only to the lips of light.

A Soldier

            (*Entering headlong on the sea-path, wounded and breathless.*)
O temple ministrants and temple guards,
Where is King Thoas? Open all your gates   1285
And call King Thoas out! Summon the king!

The First Maiden

Am I allowed to ask why so much noise?

The Soldier

The two young prisoners have broken free,
With Agamemnon's daughter joining them,   1290
And are taking Artemis aboard their ship!

The Second Maiden

You have gone mad to dream of such a thing!

The First Maiden

A likely story! If you want the king,
He has left the temple. Go and look for him.

The Soldier

Tell me which way, because I have to find him.   1295

The First Maiden

I do not know which way.

The Third Maiden

                         None of us noticed.

The Second Maiden

Go look for him, tell him your crazy story.

The Soldier

O treacherous women, you're deceiving me,
You're in the plot yourselves!   1300

The Third Maiden

                          You make no sense.
What are these men to us? Go try the palace.

The Soldier

Not till I know what's happening right here.
Not till the keepers of the inner shrine
Have answered me! Ho! You inside! Unbar
The door! Is the king there? Tell him to hurry!   1305
Tell him a soldier's out here—with bad news!

           (*He beats at the door. The door opens and Thoas appears.*)

Thoas

Why are you making this ungodly uproar?
Everyone's in a panic!

The Soldier

These women lied!
They said that you had left, they lied to me,   1310
Tried not to let me find you!

Thoas

What do you mean?
Why should they wish—

The Soldier

That will come later. Listen,
Oh listen first to me, listen to this!
Your Priestess, Iphigenia! She has freed
The prisoners! They've stolen Artemis!   1315
The ocean ceremony was a trick.

Thoas

But why should she be playing tricks on me?

The Soldier

To save Orestes. Yes, I said Orestes!

Thoas

Orestes? What Orestes? Not her brother?

The Soldier

Whom we had brought to you for Artemis.   1320

Thoas

But that's impossible! How can I grasp it?

The Soldier

There isn't time to grasp it! You must say
What's to be done about it! You must order
Galleys to cut ahead of them and catch them!

Thoas

There's no escape for them. Our boats are out there,   1325
So tell me how it happened. Everything.

The Soldier

   It was just when we had reached the bend of shore
   Hiding their ship that Agamemnon's daughter
   Made signs for us to drop the rope which bound
   The men, to leave them and fall back. She said   1330
   That she was ready to begin the rites
   And light the mystic flame to bless the sea.
   But when she took the cord and led the boys
   Beyond the curve, we had a sudden feeling
   Something was wrong. We didn't know what to do.   1335
   We heard her voice call high mysterious words
   We'd never heard and thought that this must be
   The prayer she had to use for cleansing sin.
   And then we waited a long time. At last   1340
   We were afraid the men had broken loose
   And killed her and escaped. And still we waited,
   Because you had forbidden us to look,
   But we suddenly decided to find out
   And hurried to the inlet.   1345
               There we saw
   The ship from Hellas swaying near the beach,
   And fitted in the tholes were fifty oars
   Like feathers in a wing. And the two youths
   Were waist-deep by the stern. Sailors held poles
   For keeping the bow steady, others hauled   1350
   The anchor up. The rest had hands along the ropes
   Of a ladder hanging from the rail to help
   The Priestess. But we seized her in the water,   1355
   Tugged at the ladder, ripped their rudder-oar
   Away from them to cripple them and cried
   To the fellow facing us, "What kind of man
   Are you, stealing our Priestess and our Goddess?"   1360
   "I am Orestes, son of Agamemnon,
   I am her brother! Now you have the truth!
   And she is bound for Greece, out of which land
   I lost her long ago—bound home!" We tried

To hold her, tried to drag her from their hands,   1365
Which is the way I came by this and this.
He struck my face, first one side, then the other.
They had no weapons, we had none. We used
Our fists and they their fists, and some their feet
With kicks well-aimed at us from where they stood
Above us—at our heads and hearts. We fought   1370
And fought till we were winded. Then, with bruises
And cuts and blood-filled eyes, we climbed the cliff
And from above we pelted them with rocks.   1375
But the Greek archers had brought up their bows
And with their arrows kept us at a distance.

Then when a giant wave bore in on them,
Orestes quickly lifted up his sister
Out of the rush of it. Holding her high   1380
On his left shoulder, plunging stride by stride,
He caught a ladder, climbed aboard the ship
And set her safe on deck. And she, she held—
She had it still—the statue out of Heaven,
The image of the Daughter of High Zeus.   1385

We heard a glad voice ringing through the ship,
"O mariners of Hellas, grip your oars
And clip the sea to foam! O let your arms
Be strong, for we have won, have won, have won
What we set out to win! Soon we shall leave
The jagged Clashing Rocks behind! Pull hard!"

A shout of joy resounded and the ship   1390
Quivered with dipping oars and shot ahead.
But this was only while the shelter lasted;
For at the harbor-mouth the sharp wind threw her
High on a heavy swell shoreward again.
Her oarsmen rallied, strained, but every time   1395
They made a gain, a great wave drove her back.
Then Agamemnon's daughter stood and prayed:
"Oh save me, Artemis, from this grim place!
Help us all home to Hellas! And forgive

Theft of the image at Thy Brother's bidding! 1400
As He is dear to Thee, so mine to me!"
    The sailors roared their echoes to her prayer,
And bent their bodies and their great bare arms
And shoulders, swinging like the sea,
To the boatswain's cry. But closer to the cliff, 1405
Closer they drew and closer still. And some
Sprang out into the water and began
Trying to fasten hold on the sharp rocks
With ropes. And then our soldiers sent me here
To tell you what has happened. So bring cord 1410
And chains, O King, for if the sea stays rough,
There's not a chance that they can get away.
    Poseidon, Ocean's God, mindful of Troy,
The city which He loved, is punishing 1415
The impious children of her enemies,
And will deliver to the King of Tauris
The son and daughter of the King of Argos—
That daughter who, forgetful now of Aulis,
Betrays the Goddess who was good to her.

The First Maiden

O Lady, Lady! Fate is yielding you 1420
    To Taurian hands again.
You and your brother surely now shall die.

Thoas

Come, citizens, and be uncivilized!
Leap on your horses! Whip them to the beach!
There we can wait until a billow splits
That ship from Hellas. Then go after them! 1425
And hunt them down, every damned dog of them!
Do this for Artemis. And some of you
Go launch my galleys, lest one man of them
Should die untortured! Run them down by sea
And land! Go hurl them from the cliffs!
Oh catch them, crush them, crucify them—kill them! 1430

And as for you, you miserable women,
Count on the punishment which you have earned
By treachery! That punishment can wait—
With this to do. But oh when this is done!

(*Above the confusion appears, with instant dominion,*
Pallas Athena.)

Athena

Quiet, King Thoas! What is all this tumult?   1435
Hold the chase back and listen to Athena.
Hold all your soldiers back. Yes, all of them.
    Apollo sent Orestes to your country
To set him free from the Avenging Furies,
Ordered him, through an oracle, to bring   1440
Iphigenia home again to Argos
And the sacred statue home to Her own land.
You have the story. But there's one addition—
The fact that this Orestes you would hunt
Is gliding on a comfortable sea.
Poseidon made it smooth. I asked Him to.   1445
    Orestes! Gods are heard at any distance.
Though you are far away, you still can hear me.
Do this. Take back your sister and the statue
Safely to Hellas. Pause at God-built Athens.
Then, passing through, continue to the end   1450
Of Attica and find a holy place
Close to Carystus' hill, a place called Halae.
There build a temple. There set up the image,
That men may flock to Her with happy hymns.
Name it for Tauris, to immortalize
Your flight from home, your rescue from the Furies,
Your penitence and your deliverance.   1455
    And let this be the law. When they observe
Her festival, the priest shall hold,
In memory of you, the sharp blade of his knife
Against a human throat and draw one drop   1460
Of blood, then stop—this in no disrespect

But a grave reminder of Her former ways.
   Iphigenia! Steps are cut in rock
At Brauron for a shrine to Artemis.
You shall reside as keeper of the keys there
And at your death you shall be buried there
And honored in your tomb with spotless gifts,   1465
Garments unworn, woven by hands of women
Who honorably died in giving birth.
   These loyal maidens, Thoas, I command you
To send back home.
               Orestes, once I saved you
When I was arbiter on Ares' hill   1470
And broke the tie by voting in your favor.
Now let it be the law that one who earns
An evenly divided verdict wins
His case. Therefore go safely from this land,
O son of Agamemnon. And you, Thoas,
Enjoy the taste of swallowing your wrath.

Thoas

The man who thinks he ever stood a chance   1475
Against the Gods was born a fool. And so
I hold no slightest grievance toward Orestes
Or Iphigenia. They may keep the statue.
There isn't even any dignity
In challenging a God. So off with them.   1480
May Artemis be happy in their land.
   I bid these women also, since I have to,
A pleasant trip to Hellas. Thy word holds
For all my captains too. Call back the galleys!
Here are my spirit—and my spear—bowed down.   1485

Athena

In doing as you must, you learn a law
Binding on Gods as well as upon men.
   O winds of Heaven, speed Orestes home,

And I will guide him on his way to Athens
And will save Thy likeness, Artemis, my Sister.

The First Maiden
    Smooth seas to them and may their journey's end   1490
        Become unending joy!

The Fourth Maiden
    Pallas Athena, let us prove Thy name
    As hallowed upon earth as in high Heaven.

The Third Maiden
        And let us take to heart
    Thy unexpected but so welcome words.   1495

The Second Maiden
        Command us with Thy grace,
    O Conqueror of anger and of fear,
        Award us wiser ways.

The First Maiden
    Undo our troubled guile, crown us with Truth.   1499

ELECTRA

Translated by Emily Townsend Vermeule

INTRODUCTION

Electra is usually dated 413 B.C., since the Dioscuri at the end are thought to be alluding to the relief fleet sent from Athens to Sicily in that year. This is very likely, though not quite certain. I take the *Electra* of Euripides to be subsequent to that of Sophocles. This seems to be the majority view, but here again certainty is lacking.

Euripides may have proposed to carry the realistic approach of Sophocles a stage further. How could this murder, how would it in fact, have been done? The recognition scene of Aeschylus is deliberately mocked, and a more plausible one substituted. The difficulty of entering the palace and eluding the palace guards is avoided by setting the scene in the country, near the frontiers of the kingdom. There Electra lives, married to a humble but honorable farmer, her husband in name only. There Orestes, a nervous homicide, lurks, concealing his identity until he is recognized, apparently against his will. There Aegisthus and Clytemnestra, separately, are set upon and killed. The villains are not, it seems, quite so bad as they have been made out to be. A courteous Aegisthus is hewn down while he is being hospitable to strangers. Clytemnestra is more vain and weak than malignant, she is not happy over her career, and she is murdered while performing an act of kindness. Orestes lacks heroic stature; Electra, sorry for herself and making an exhibition of her mistreatment, seems an all too lifelike parody of her tragic predecessors. Castor and Polydeuces, the "Dioscuri" or heavenly twins (Clytemnestra's brothers), appear aloft at the end as *deus ex machina*. They answer, possibly, Sophocles; they accept what has been done, but disapprove (lines 1244–46):

> Justice has claimed her, but you have not worked in justice.
> As for Phoebus, Phoebus—yet he is my lord,
> silence. He knows the truth but his oracles were lies.

Violence as the answer to violence is no solution.

This somewhat repellent action is relieved by odes of considerable lyric grace, which do not always bear directly on the story.

NOTE

The text followed is J. D. Denniston's Oxford edition (1939), based on Murray. Lines 899 and 1097-1101 (= fragment 464, *Cretan Women*) have been omitted, and the order of speakers at 677-81 has been changed to accord with Denniston's tentative suggestion.

CHARACTERS

Farmer, a Mycenaean

Electra

Orestes

Pylades, a mute character

Chorus of Argive peasant women

Old Man

Messenger

Clytemnestra

Dioscuri: Castor, and Polydeuces, a mute character

ELECTRA

SCENE: *A high bare slope of the Argive hills commanding a view of the road to Argos, stage left, and the southern passes toward Sparta, right. A square timber-and-mudbrick cottage stands in the center. The time is the end of night with stars still in the sky. The Farmer stands looking down toward the river valley and the sea.*

Farmer

Argos, old bright floor of the world, Inachus' pouring
tides—King Agamemnon once on a thousand ships
hoisted the war god here and sailed across to Troy.
He killed the monarch of the land of Ilium,
Priam; he sacked the glorious city of Dardanus;   5
he came home safe to Argos and high on the towering shrines
nailed up the massive loot of Barbary for the gods.
So, over there he did well. But in his own house
he died in ambush planned for him by his own wife
Clytemnestra and by her lover Aegisthus' hand.   10
    He lost the ancient scepter of Tantalus; he is dead.
Thyestes' son Aegisthus walks king in the land
and keeps the dead man's wife for himself, Tyndareus' child.
As for the children he left home when he sailed to Troy,
his son Orestes and his flowering girl Electra,   15
Orestes almost died under Aegisthus' fist,
but his father's ancient servant snatched the boy away,
gave him to Strophius to bring up in the land of Phocis.
Electra waited motionless in her father's house.
But when the burning season of young ripeness took her,   20
then the great princes of the land of Greece came begging
her bridal. Aegisthus was afraid. Afraid her son
if noble in blood would punish Agamemnon's death.
He held her in the house sundered from every love.
Yet, even guarded so, she filled his nights with fear   25
lest she in secret to some prince might still bear sons;

he laid his plans to kill her. But her mother, though
savage in soul, then saved her from Aegisthus' blow.
The lady found excuse for murdering her husband
but flinched from killing a child, afraid of the world's contempt.   30
Later Aegisthus framed a new design. He swore
to any man who captured Agamemnon's son
running in exile and murdered him, a price of gold.
Electra—he gave her to me as a gift, to hold
her as my wife.

        Now, I was born of Mycenaean   35
family, on this ground I have nothing to be ashamed of,
in breeding they shone bright enough. But in their fortune
they ranked as paupers, which blots out all decent blood.
He gave her to me, a weak man, to weaken his own fear,
for if a man of high position had taken her   40
he might have roused awake the sleeping Agamemnon's
blood—justice might have knocked at Aegisthus' door.
I have not touched her and the love-god Cypris knows it:
I never shamed the girl in bed, she is still virgin.
I would feel ugly holding down the gentle daughter   45
of a king in violence, I was not bred to such an honor.
And poor laboring Orestes whom they call my brother—
I suffer his grief, I think his thoughts, if he came home
to Argos and saw his sister so doomed in her wedding.
Whoever says that I am a born fool to keep   50
a young girl in my house and never touch her body,
or says I measure wisdom by a crooked line
of morals, should know he is as great a fool as I.

        *(Electra enters from the cottage carrying a water jar on
                her head and talking to herself.)*

Electra

O night, black night, whose breast nurses the golden stars,
I wander through your darkness, head lifted to bear   55
this pot I carry to the sources of the river—
I am not forced, I chose this slavery myself

to illuminate Aegisthus' arrogance for the gods—
and cry my pain to Father in the great bright air.
For my own mother, she, Tyndareus' deadly daughter,   60
has thrown me out like dirt from the house, to her husband's joy,
and while she breeds new children in Aegisthus' bed
has made me and Orestes aliens to her love.

Farmer

Now why, unhappy girl, must you for my sake wrestle
such heavy work though you were raised in luxury?   65
Each time I mention it you flash into rebellion.

Electra

I think you equal to the gods in kindliness,
for you have never hurt me though I am in trouble.
It is great fortune for men to find a kind physician
of suffering, which I have found in finding you.   70
Indeed without your bidding I should make the labor
as light as I have strength for; you will bear it better
if I claim some share with you in the work. Outdoors
you have enough to do; my place is in the house,
to keep it tidy. When a man comes in from work   75
it is sweet to find his hearthplace looking swept and clean.

Farmer

Well, if your heart is set on helping, go. The spring
is not so distant from the house. At light of dawn
I will put the cows to pasture and start planting the fields.
A lazy man may rustle gods upon his tongue   80
but never makes a living if he will not work.

> (*They go off together, stage right. Enter Orestes and Pylades
> from the mountain road, quickly but cautiously, and as-
> sure themselves the coast is clear.*)

Orestes

Pylades, I consider you the first of men
in loyalty and love to me, my host and friend.

You only of my friends gave honor and respect
to Orestes, suffering as I suffer from Aegisthus.   85
He killed my father—he and my destructive mother.
I come from secret converse with the holy god
to this outpost of Argos—no one knows I am here—
to counterchange my father's death for death to his killers.
During the night just passed I found my father's tomb,   90
gave him my tears in gift and sheared my hair in mourning
and sprinkled ceremonial sheep's blood on the fire,
holding the rite concealed from the tyrants who rule here.

I will not set my foot inside the city walls.
I chose this gatepost of the land deliberately,   95
compacting a double purpose. First, if any spy
should recognize me I can run for foreign soil,
second, to find my sister. For they say she married
and, tamed to domestic love, lives here no longer virgin.
I want to be with her and take her as my partner   100
in the work and learn precise news from behind the walls.

And now, since lady dawn is lifting her white face,
smooth out our footprints from the path and come away.
Perhaps a field-bound farmer or some cottage wife
will meet us on the road, and we can ask discreetly   105
whether my sister lives anywhere in these hills.

Quick now! I see some sort of serving girl approach
with a jar of fountain water on her shaven head—
it looks heavy for her. Sit down here, let us question
the slave girl. Pylades, perhaps at last we shall hear   110
the news we hoped for when we crossed into this land.

> (*They hide behind the altar in front of the cottage. Electra*
> *comes back along the path with her jar, singing*
> *aloud, half dancing.*)

Electra

Quicken the foot's rush—time has struck—O
walk now, walk now weeping aloud,
        O for my grief!

I was bred Agamemnon's child,   115
formed in the flesh of Clytemnestra
   Tyndareus' hellish daughter,
Argos' people have named me true:
      wretched Electra.
Cry, cry for my labor and pain,   120
   cry for the hatred of living.
Father who in the halls of death
lie hacked by your wife and Aegisthus, O
   help, Agamemnon!

Come, waken the mourning again,   125
bring me again the sweetness of tears.

Quicken the foot's rush—time has struck—O
walk now, walk now weeping aloud,
     O for my grief!
In what city and in what house, O   130
brother of grief, do you walk a slave?
   You left me locked in the cursed
palace chambers for doom to strike
     your sister in sorrow.
Come, loose me from labor, come   135
   save me in pity, O Zeus,
Zeus, for our father's hate-spilled blood
help storm the wicked and harbor our lost
     voyager in Argos.

Set this vessel down from my head, O   140
take it, while I lift music of mourning
    by night to my father.
Father, the maenad song of death
   I cry you among the dead
beneath the earth, the words I pour   145
    day after day unending
as I move, ripping my flesh with sharp

nails, fists pounding my clipped
    head for your dying.

Ai, ai, tear my face!   150
I, like the swan of echoing song
in descant note at the water's edge
who calls to its parent so dearly loved
and dying now in the hidden net
of twisted meshes, mourn you thus   155
    in agony dying,

body steeped in the final bath,
lull most pitiful, sleep of death.
    O for my grief!
Bitter the ax and bitter the gash,   160
  bitter the road you walked
from Troy straight to their plotted net—
  your lady did not receive you
with victor's ribbons or flowers to crown you,
but with double-edged steel she made you
savage sport for Aegisthus, gave you   165
    to her shifty lover.

           (*The chorus of Argive peasant women enters from the
                Mycenae road to confront Electra.*)

Chorus

  Princess, daughter of Agamemnon,
  we have come to your country court,
      Electra, to see you.
  There passed, passed me a man
      bred on the milk of the hills,
  a Mycenaean mountaineer   170
  who gave me word that on the third
  day the Argives herald abroad
  a holy feast, when all the girls
  will pass in procession up to the temple of Hera.

Electra

    Dear friends, not for shimmering robes,   175
    not for twisted bracelets of gold
        does my heart take wing in delight.
    I am too sad, I cannot stand
        in choral joy with the maidens
    or beat the tune with my whirling foot;   180
        rather with tears by night
    and tears by day shall I fill my soul
        shaking in grief and fear.
    Look! think! would my filthy locks
    and robe all torn into slavish rags   185
    do public honor to Agamemnon's
        daughter, the princess?
    honor to Troy which will never forget
        my conquering father?

Chorus

    Great, great is the goddess. Come,   190
    I will lend you a dress to wear,
        thick-woven of wool,
    and gold—be gracious, accept—
                      gold for holiday glitter.
    Do you think your tears and holding back
    honor from god will ever hurt   195
    your haters? Not by sounding lament
    but only by prayer and reverent love
    for the gods, my child, will you learn to live gentler days.

Electra

    Gods? Not one god has heard
    my helpless cry or watched of old   200
        over my murdered father.
    Mourn again for the wasted dead,
        mourn for the living outlaw

somewhere prisoned in foreign lands
  moving through empty days,
passing from one slave hearth to the next   205
  though born of a glorious sire.
And I! I in a peasant's hut
waste my life like wax in the sun,
thrust and barred from my father's home
  to a scarred mountain exile   210
while my mother rolls in her bloody bed
  and plays at love with a stranger.

Chorus

Like Helen, your mother's sister—Helen charged and found
guilty of massive pain to Greece and all your house.

Electra

Oh, oh! women, I break from my deathbound cry.   215
Look! there are strangers here close to the house who crouch
huddled beside the altar and rise up in ambush.
Run, you take the path and I into the house
with one swift rush can still escape these criminals.

Orestes

Poor girl, stand still, and fear not. I would never hurt you.   220

Electra

Phoebus Apollo, help! I kneel to you. Do not kill me.

Orestes

I hope I shall kill others hated more than you.

Electra

Get out; don't touch. You have no right to touch my body.

Orestes

There is no person I could touch with greater right.

Electra

Why were you hiding, sword in hand, so near my house?   225

Orestes

Stand still and listen. You will agree I have rights here.

Electra

I stand here utterly in your power. You are stronger.

Orestes

I have come to bring you a spoken message from your brother.

Electra

Dearest of strangers, is he alive or is he dead?

Orestes

Alive. I wish to give you all the best news first.   230

Electra

God bless your days, as you deserve for such sweet words.

Orestes

I share your gift with you that we may both be blessed.

Electra

Where is he now, attempting to bear unbearable exile?

Orestes

He is wrecked, nor can conform to any city's code.

Electra

Tell me, he is not poor? not hungry for daily bread?   235

Orestes

He has bread, yet he has the exile's constant hunger.

Electra

You came to bring a message—what are his words for me?

Orestes

"Are you alive? Where are you living? What is your life?"

Electra

I think you see me. First, my body wasted and dry—

Orestes

Sadness has wasted you so greatly I could weep.   240

Electra

Next, my head razor-cropped like a victim of the Scythians.

Orestes

Your brother's life and father's death both bite at your heart.

Electra

Alas, what else have I? I have no other loves.

Orestes

You grieve me. Whom do you think your brother loves but you?

Electra

He is not here. He loves me, but he is not here.   245

Orestes

Why do you live in a place like this, so far from town?

Electra

Because I married, stranger—a wedding much like death.

Orestes

Bad news for your brother. Your husband is a Mycenaean?

Electra

But not the man my father would have wished me to marry.

Orestes

Tell me. I am listening, I can speak to your brother.   250

Electra

This is his house. I live quite isolated here.

Orestes

A ditch-digger, a cowherd would look well living here.

Electra

He is a poor man but well born, and he respects me.

Orestes

Respects? What does your husband understand by "respect"?

Electra

He has never been violent or touched me in my bed.   255

Orestes

A vow of chastity? or he finds you unattractive?

Electra

He finds it attractive not to insult my royal blood.

Orestes

How could he not be pleased at marrying so well?

Electra

He judges the man who gave me had no right to, stranger.

Orestes

I see—afraid Orestes might avenge your honor.   260

Electra

Afraid of that, yes—he is also decent by nature.

Orestes

Ah.
You paint one of nature's gentlemen. We must pay him well.

Electra

We will, if my absent brother ever gets home again.

Orestes

Your mother took the wedding calmly, I suppose?

Electra

Women save all their love for lovers, not for children.   265

Orestes

What was in Aegisthus' mind, to insult you so?

Electra

He hoped that I, so wedded, would have worthless sons.

Orestes

Too weak for undertaking blood-revenge on him?

Electra

That was his hope. I hope to make him pay for it.

Orestes

This husband of your mother's—does he know you are virgin?   270

Electra

No, he knows nothing. We have played our parts in silence.

Orestes

These women listening as we talk are friends of yours?

Electra

Good enough friends to keep our words kindly concealed.

Orestes

How should Orestes play *his* part, if he comes to Argos?

Electra

If he comes? ugly talk. The time has long been ripe.   275

Orestes

Say he comes, still how could he kill his father's killers?

Electra

As Father suffered let our enemies suffer too.

Orestes

Mother and lover both? are you bold for that killing?

Electra

Mother by the same ax that cut Father to ruin.

Orestes

May I tell him what you say and how determined you are?   280

Electra

Tell him how gladly I would die in Mother's blood.

Orestes

O, I wish Orestes could stand here and listen.

Electra

Yet if I saw him I should hardly know him, sir.

Orestes

No wonder. You were both very young when you were parted.

Electra

I have only one friend who might still know his face.   285

Orestes

The man who saved him once from death, as the story goes?

Electra

Yes, old now and old even when he nursed my father.

Orestes

When your father died did his body find some burial?

Electra

He found what he found. He was thrown on the dirt outdoors.

Orestes

    I cannot bear it. What have you said? Even a stranger's   290
pain bites strangely deep and hurts us when we hear it.
Tell me the rest, and with new knowledge I will bring
Orestes your tale, so harsh to hear and so compelling
when heard. Uneducated men are pitiless,
but we who are educated pity much. And we pay   295
a high price for being intelligent. Wisdom hurts.

Chorus

    The same excitement stirs my mind in this as yours—
I live far from the city and I know its troubles
hardly at all. Now I would like to learn them too.

Electra

    I will tell if I must—and must tell you who love me—   300
how my luck, and my father's, is too heavy to lift.
Since you have moved me to speak so, stranger, I must beg
that you will tell Orestes all my distress, and his.
First tell him how I am kept like a beast in stable rags,
my skin heavy with grease and dirt. Describe to him   305
this hut—*my* home, who used to live in the king's palace.
I weave my clothes myself and slavelike at the loom
must work or else walk naked through the world in nothing.
I fetch and carry water from the riverside,
I am deprived of holy festivals and dances,   310
I cannot talk to women since I am a girl,
I cannot think of Castor, who was close in blood
and loved me once, before he rose among the gods.
My mother in the glory of her Phrygian rugs
sits on the throne, while circled at her feet the girls   315
of Asia stoop, whom Father won at the sack of Troy,
their clothes woven in snowy wool from Ida, pinned
with golden brooches, while the walls and floor are stained
still with my father's black and rotting blood. The man
who murdered him goes riding grand in Father's chariot,   320

with bloody hands and high delight lifting the staff
of office by which Father marshaled the Greek lords.
The tomb of Agamemnon finds no honor yet,
never yet drenched with holy liquids or made green
in myrtle branches, barren of bright sacrifice.   325
But in his drunken fits, my mother's lover, brilliant
man, triumphant leaps and dances on the mound
or pelts my father's stone memorial with rocks
and dares to shout against us with his boldened tongue:
"Where is your son Orestes? When will that noble youth   330
come to protect your tomb?" Insults to empty space.
  Kind stranger, as I ask you, tell him all these things.
For many call him home again—I speak for them—
the voices in our hands and tongues and grieving minds
and heads, shaven in mourning; and his father calls.   335
All will be shamed if he whose father captured Troy
cannot in single courage kill a single man,
although his strength is younger and his blood more noble.

Chorus

Electra! I can see your husband on the road.
He has finished his field work and is coming home.   340

> (*The Farmer enters from the left to con-
> front the group by his house.*)

Farmer

Hey there! who are these strangers standing at our gates?
What is the errand that could bring them to our rough
courtyard? Are they demanding something from me? A nice
woman should never stand in gossip with young men.

Electra

My dearest husband, do not come suspecting me.   345
You shall hear their story, the whole truth. They come
as heralds to me with new tidings of Orestes.
Strangers, I ask you to forgive him what he said.

Farmer

What news? Is Orestes still alive in the bright light?

Electra

So they have told me, and I do not doubt their words.   350

Farmer

Does he still remember his father, and your troubles?

Electra

We hope so. But an exile is a helpless man.

Farmer

Then what are these plans of his? What have they come to tell?

Electra

He sent them simply to see my troubles for themselves.

Farmer

What they don't see themselves I imagine you have told them.   355

Electra

They know it all. I took good care that they missed nothing.

Farmer

Why were our doors not opened to them long ago?
Move into the house, you will find entertainment
to answer your good news, such as my roof can offer.
Servants, pick up their baggage, bring their spears indoors.   360
Come, no polite refusals. You are here as friends
most dear to me who meet you now. Though I am poor
in money, I think you will not find our manners poor.

Orestes

By the gods! is this the man who helps you keep your marriage
a fiction, who has no desire to shame Orestes?   365

Electra

This is the man they know as poor Electra's husband.

Orestes

Alas,
we look for good on earth and cannot recognize it
when met, since all our human heritage runs mongrel.
At times I have seen descendants of the noblest family
grow worthless though the cowards had courageous sons;   370
inside the souls of wealthy men bleak famine lives
while minds of stature struggle trapped in starving bodies.
    How then can man distinguish man, what test can he use?
the test of wealth? that measure means poverty of mind;
of poverty? the pauper owns one thing, the sickness   375
of his condition, a compelling teacher of evil;
by nerve in war? yet who, when a spear is cast across
his face, will stand to witness his companion's courage?
We can only toss our judgments random on the wind.
    This fellow here is no great man among the Argives,   380
not dignified by family in the eyes of the world—
he is a face in the crowd, and yet we choose him champion.
Can you not come to understand, you empty-minded,
opinion-stuffed people, a man is judged by grace
among his fellows, manners are nobility's touchstone?   385
Such men of manners can control our cities best,
and homes, but the well-born sportsman, long on muscle, short
on brains, is only good for a statue in the park,
not even sterner in the shocks of war than weaker
men, for courage is the gift of character.   390
    Now let us take whatever rest this house can give;
Agamemnon's child deserves it, the one here and the one
absent for whom I stand. We have no choice but go
indoors, servants, inside the house, since our poor host
seems eager to entertain us, more than a rich man might.   395
I do praise and admire his most kind reception
but would have been more pleased if your brother on the crest

of fortune could have brought me to a more fortunate house.
Perhaps he may still come; Apollo's oracles
are strong, though human prophecy is best ignored.   400

(Orestes and Pylades go into the house.)

Chorus

Now more than ever in our lives, Electra, joy
makes our hearts light and warm. Perhaps your fortune, first
running these painful steps, will stride to the goal in glory.

Electra

You are thoughtless. You know quite well the house is bare;
why take these strangers in? They are better born than you.   405

Farmer

Why? Because if they are the gentlemen they seem,
will they not treat the small as gently as the great?

Electra

Small is the word for you. Now the mistake is made,
go quickly to my father's loved and ancient servant
who by Tanaos' river, where it cuts the hills   410
of Argos off from Spartan country, goes his rounds
watching his flocks in distant exile from the town.
Tell him these strangers have descended on me; ask
him to come and bring some food fit for distinguished guests.
He will surely be happy; he will bless the gods   415
when he hears the child he saved so long ago still lives.
Besides, we cannot get any help from Father's house,
from Mother—our news would fly to her on bitter wings,
bold though she is, if she should hear Orestes lives.

Farmer

Well, if you wish it, I can pass your message on   420
to the old man. But you get quick into the house
and ready up what's there. A woman when she has to
can always find some food to set a decent table.

(Electra goes into the cottage.)

The house holds little, yet it is enough, I know,
to keep these strangers choked with food at least one day.   425
    In times like these, when wishes soar but power fails,
I contemplate the steady comfort found in gold:
gold you can spend on guests; gold you can pay the doctor
when you get sick. But a small crumb of gold will buy
our daily bread, and when a man has eaten that,   430
you cannot really tell the rich and poor apart.

                    (*The farmer goes off right, toward the hills.*)
Chorus
    O glorious ships who sailed across to Troy once
        moving on infinite wooden oars
    guarding the circling choir of Nereid dancers
    where the dolphin shook in love at the flute-   435
        melody and about the sea-
        blue prows went plunging
    as he led the goddess Thetis' son,
    light-striding Achilles, on his way
    with Agamemnon to Ilium's cliffs   440
        where Simois pours in the sea.

    Of old the Nereids passed Euboea's headlands
        bringing the heavy shield of gold,
    forged on Hephaestus' anvil, and golden armor.
    Up Mount Pelion, up the jut   445
        of Ossa's holy slopes on high,
        up the nymphs' spy-rocks
    they hunted the aged horseman's hill
    where he trained the boy as a dawn for Greece,
    the son of Thetis, sea-bred and swift-   450
        lived in the Atreid wars.

    Once I heard from a Trojan captive known to the port
        in Nauplia close to Argos
        of your brilliant shield, O goddess'
    child, how in its circled space   455

these signs, scenes, were in blazon warning,
   mourning, for Phrygia:
running in frieze on its massive rim,
Perseus lifting the severed head
cut at the neck—with Gorgon beauty   460
he walks on wings over the sea;
Hermes is with him, angel of Zeus,
   great Maia's
child of the flocks and forests.

Out of the shield's curved center glittered afar the high
   shining round of the sun   465
      driving with wingèd horses,
and the chorused stars of upper air—
Pleiads, Hyads—Hector eyed them,
   swerving aside.
Over the helmet of beaten gold   470
Sphinxes snatch in hooking nails
their prey trapped with song. On the hollow
greave, the lioness' fire breath
flares in her clawed track as she runs,
   staring back
at the wind-borne foal of Peirene.   475

All along the blade of the deadly sword, hooves pounding,
horses leap; black above their backs the dust blows.
   Still this prince of arms and men
   you killed by lust of sex and sin   480
   of mind, Tyndarid Helen.
For this the sons of heaven will send
you yet among the dead; some far
day I shall still see your blood fall   485
red from your neck on the iron sword.

               (Enter the Old Man, alone, from the right,
                     out of breath after climbing.)

Old Man

    Where is my young mistress and my lady queen,
the child of Agamemnon, whom I raised and loved?
How steep this house seems set to me, with rough approach,
as I grow old for climbing on this withered leg.   490
But when your friends call, you must come and drag along
and hump your spine till it snaps and bend your knees like pins.

                        (Electra enters from the cottage.)

    Why there she is—my daughter, look at you by the door!
I am here. I have brought you from my cropping sheep
a newborn lamb, a tender one, just pulled from the teat,   495
and flowers looped in garlands, cheese white from the churn,
and this stored treasure of the wine god, aged and spiked
with a pungent smell—not much of it, but sweet, and good
to pour into the cup with other weaker wine.
Let someone carry all this gear to the guests indoors,   500
for I have cried a little and would like to dry
my face and eyes out here on my cloak—more holes than wool.

Electra

    Old uncle, father, why is your face so stained with tears?
After so long has my grief stirred your thoughts again,
or is it poor Orestes in his running days   505
you mourn for, or my father, whom your two old hands
once nursed and helped without reward for self or love?

Old Man

    Reward, no. Yet I could not stop myself, in this:
for I came past his tomb and circled from the road
and fell to the earth there, weeping for its loneliness,   510
and let it drink, tapping this winesack for your guests
in brief libation, and I wreathed the stone in myrtle.
And there I saw on the burning-altar a black-fleeced
sheep, throat cut and blood still warm in its dark stream,
and curling locks of bright brown hair cut off in gift.   515

I stopped, quiet, to wonder, child, what man had courage
to visit at that tomb. It could not be an Argive.
    Is there a chance your brother has arrived in secret
and paused to stare upon his father's shabby tomb?
Look at the lock of hair, match it to your own head,   520
see if it is not twin to yours in color and cut.
Often a father's blood, running in separate veins,
makes the two bodies almost mirrors in their form.

Electra

Old man, I always thought you were wiser than you sound
if you really think my brother, who is bright and bold,   525
would come to our land in hiding, frightened by Aegisthus.
Besides, how could a lock of his hair match with mine?
one from a man with rugged training in the ring
and games, one combed and girlish? It is not possible.
You may find many matching birds of the same feather   530
not bred in the same nest, old man, nor matched in blood.

Old Man

At least go set your foot in the print of his hunting boot
and see if it is not the same as yours, my child.

Electra

You make me angry. How could rocky ground receive
the imprint of a foot? And if it could be traced,   535
it would not be the same for brother and for sister,
a man's foot and a girl's—of course his would be bigger.

Old Man

Is there no sign then, if your brother should come home...
of loom or pattern by which you would know the cloth
you wove, I wrapped him in, to rescue him from death?   540

Electra

You know quite well Orestes went away in exile
when I was very small. If a little girl's hand

could weave, how could a growing boy still wear that cloth
unless his shirt and tunic lengthened with his legs?

Some pitying stranger must have passed the tomb and cut   545
a mourning-lock, or townsmen slipping past the spies. . . .

Old Man

Where are the strangers now? I want to look them over
and draw them out with conversation of your brother.

(*Orestes and Pylades enter from the cottage.*)

Electra

Here they come striding lightly from the cottage now.

Old Man

Well. They look highborn enough, but the coin may prove   550
false. Often a noble face hides filthy ways.
Nevertheless—
                    Greetings, strangers, I wish you well.

Orestes

And greetings in return, old sir.
                              Electra, where,
to what friends of yours, does this human antique belong?

Electra

This is the man who nursed and loved my father, sir.   555

Orestes

What! the one who saved your brother once from death?

Electra

Indeed he saved him—if indeed he still is safe.

Orestes

Ah, so!
Why do you stare upon me like a man who squints
at the bright stamp of a coin? Do I stir your memory?

Electra

Perhaps just happy seeing Orestes' twin in age.   560

Orestes

Dear Orestes. Why does he walk round me in circles?

Electra

Stranger, I am astonished too as I look at him.

Old Man

Mistress, now pray. Daughter Electra, pray to the gods.

Electra

For what of the things I have, or all I never had?

Old Man

For a treasure of love within your grasp, which god reveals.   565

Electra

As you please; I will pray the gods. What was in your mind?

Old Man

Look now upon this man, my child—your dearest love.

Electra

I have been looking rather at you; is your mind disturbed?

Old Man

My mind not steady when my eyes have seen your brother?

Electra

What have you said, old man? what hopeless impossible word?   570

Old Man

I said I see Orestes—here—Agamemnon's son.

Electra

How? What sign do you see? What can I know and trust?

Old Man

The scar above his eye where once he slipped and drew
blood as he helped you chase a fawn in your father's court.

Electra

I see the mark of a fall, but—I cannot believe—   575

Old Man

How long will you stand, hold yourself back from his arms and
    love?

Electra

I will not any longer, for my heart has trust
in the token you show.
                        O Brother so delayed by time,
I hold you against hope—

Orestes

                        Time hid you long from me.

Electra

I never promised myself—

Orestes

                        I had abandoned hope.   580

Electra

And are you he?

Orestes

                I am, your sole defender and friend.
Now if I catch the prey for which I cast my net—

Electra

I trust you and trust in you. Never believe in god
again if evil can still triumph over good.

Chorus

You have come, you have come, our slow, bright day,   585
    you have shone, you have shown a beacon-

lit hope for the state, who fled of old
your father's palace, doomed and pained,
    drifting in exile.

Now god, some god restores us strong   590
   to triumph, my love.
Lift high your hands, lift high your voice, raise
prayers to the gods. In fortune, fortune
your brother shall march straight to the city's heart.   595

Orestes

   Enough. I find sweet pleasure in embrace and welcome,
but let us give ourselves over to pleasure later.
Old man, you came on the crest of opportunity—
tell me what I must do to punish the murderer
and purify my mother from adultery.   600
Have I in Argos any strong measure of friends
or am I bankrupt in backing as I am in fortune?
Whom shall I look to? Shall it be by day or night?
What hunting-track will lead me toward my enemies?

Old Man

   My son, you lost your friends when luck deserted you.   605
That would indeed be luck met on the road for you,
someone to share both good and evil without change.
But you from root to leaf-top have been robbed of friends
who, leaving, left you no bequest of hope. Hear me:
in your own hand and the grace of god you hold all poised   610
to capture back your city, place, and patrimony.

Orestes

   But what should we be doing now to strike our target?

Old Man

   Kill him. Kill Thyestes' son. And kill your mother.

Orestes

   Such the triumphal crown I came for, yet—how reach it?

Old Man

    Not inside the city even if you were willing.   615

Orestes

    Is he so strongly fenced by bodyguards and spears?

Old Man

    You know it. The man's afraid of you and cannot sleep.

Orestes

    Let that go, then. Tell me another way, old man.

Old Man

    Yes—you shall hear, for something came to me just now.

Orestes

    I hope your plan and my reaction are equally good.   620

Old Man

    I saw Aegisthus as I hauled my way up here.

Orestes

    Good, that sounds hopeful. Where am I to find him now?

Old Man

    Close, down in the meadows where his horses graze.

Orestes

    What is he doing? Out of despair I see new light.

Old Man

    Offering a banquet to the goddess Nymphs, I think.   625

Orestes

    To keep his children safe? For a child soon to be born?

Old Man

    I know only that he is prepared to kill a bull.

Orestes

How many men are with him? simply alone with servants?

Old Man

No citizens were there; a handful of palace servants.

Orestes

No one who might still recognize my face, old man?   630

Old Man

They are his private servants and have never seen you.

Orestes

And would they, if we conquered, be, ah—kindly disposed?

Old Man

That is characteristic of slaves, and luck for you.

Orestes

How would you suggest my getting close to him?

Old Man

Walk past where he will see you as he sacrifices.   635

Orestes

He has his fields, I gather, right beside this road?

Old Man

And when he sees you he will ask you to join the feast.

Orestes

He shall find a bitter banquet-fellow, if god wills.

Old Man

What happens next—you play it as the dice may fall.

Orestes

Well spoken. The woman who gave me birth is—where?   640

Old Man

In Argos. She will join her husband for the feast.

Orestes

But why did she—my mother—not start out with him?

Old Man

The gossip of the crowd disturbs her. She held back.

Orestes

Of course. She feels the city watching her on the sly.

Old Man

That's how it is. Everyone hates a promiscuous wife.   645

Orestes

Then how can I kill them both at the same time and place?

(Electra comes forward.)

Electra

I will be the one to plan my mother's death.

Orestes

Good—then fortune will arrange the first death well.

Electra

Let our single friend here help us with both deaths.

Old Man

It shall be done. What death have you decided for her?   650

Electra

Old uncle, you must go to Clytemnestra; tell her
that I am kept in bed after bearing a son.

Old Man

Some time ago? or has your baby just arrived?

Electra

Ten days ago, which days I have kept ritually clean.

Old Man

And how will this achieve the murder of your mother? 655

Electra

She will come, of course, when she hears about the birth.

Old Man

Why? Do you think she cares so deeply for you, child?

Electra

Yes—and she can weep about the boy's low breeding.

Old Man

Perhaps. Return now to the goal of your design.

Electra

She will come; she will be killed. All that is clear. 660

Old Man

I see—she comes and walks directly in your door.

Electra

From there she need walk only a short way, to death.

Old Man

I will gladly die too, when I have seen her die.

Electra

But first, old man, you ought to guide Orestes down—

Old Man

Where Aegisthus holds his sacrifices to the gods? 665

Electra

Then go face my mother, tell her all about me.

Old Man

    I'll speak so well she'll think it is Electra speaking.

Electra (to Orestes)

    Your task is ready. You have drawn first chance at murder.

Orestes

    Well, I would go if anyone could show me where.

Old Man

    I will escort you on your way with greatest joy.   670

Orestes

    O Zeus of Our Fathers, now be Router of Foes.

Electra

    Have pity on us, for our days are piteous.

Old Man

    Pity them truly—children sprung of your own blood.

Electra

    O Hera, holy mistress of Mycenae's altars—

Orestes

    Grant us the victory if our claim to victory is just.   675

Old Man

    Grant them at last avenging justice for their father.

Electra

    O Earth, ruler below, to whom I stretch my hands—

Orestes

    And you, O Father, dwelling wronged beneath the earth—

Old Man

    Protect, protect these children here, so dearly loved.

Electra

Come now and bring as army all the dead below— 680

Orestes

Who stood beside you at Troy with the havoc of their spears—

Old Man

All who hate the godless guilty defilers here.

Electra

Did you hear us, terrible victim of our mother's love?

Old Man

All, your father hears all, I know. Time now to march.

Electra

I call to you again and say *Aegisthus dies!* 685
And if Orestes in his struggle falls to death
I too am dead, let them no longer say I live,
for I will stab my belly with a two-edged sword.
    I will go in and make our dwelling fit for the outcome:
then if a message of good fortune comes from you 690
the whole house shall ring out in triumph. If you die
triumph will shift to desolation. This is my word.

Orestes

I understand you.

Electra

                    Make yourself fit man for the hour.
You, my women, with your voices light a fire-
signal of shouting in this trial. I shall stand guard, 695
a sword raised ready for the issue in my hand.
Even in defeat I shall not grant to those
I hate, the right to violate my living flesh.

> (*Orestes, the Old Man, and Pylades go off toward
> Mycenae; Electra withdraws into the house.*)

Chorus

> The ancient tale is told
>> in Argos
> still—how a magic lamb   700
> from its mother gay on the hills
> Pan stole, Pan of the wild
> beasts, kind watcher, Pan
> who breathes sweet music to his jointed reed.
> He brought it to show the gold   705
> curls of its wool. On the stone
> steps a standing herald called:
> *To the square, to the square, you men*
> *of Mycenae! Come, run, behold*
>> *a strange and lovely thing*   710
> *for our blessed kings.* Swiftly the chorus in dance
>> beat out honor to Atreus' house.

> The altars spread their wings
>> of hammered
> gold, fire gleamed in the town
> like the moon on Argos' stones   715
> of sacrifice, lotus flutes
> tended the Muses, lilting
> ripples of tune. The dance swelled in desire
> tense for the lamb of gold—
> whose? Quick, Thyestes' trick:
> seducing in the dark of sleep   720
> Atreus' wife, he brought
> the strange lamb home, his own.
>> Back to the square he calls
> all to know how he holds the golden beast,
>> fleece and horn, from Atreus' house.   725

> That hour—that hour Zeus
> changed the stars on their blazing course,
> utterly turned the splendid sun,

turned the white face of the dawn   730
so the sun drives west over heaven's spine
    in glowing god-lit fire,
the watery weight of cloud moves north,
the cracked waste of African Ammon
dries up, dies, never knowing dew,   735
robbed of the beautiful rain that drops from Zeus.

Thus it is always told.
I am won only to light belief
that the sun would swerve or change his gold
chamber of fire, moved in pain   740
at sorrow and sin in the mortal world,
    to judge or punish man.
Yet terrible myths are gifts
which call men to the worship of god.
You lost god when you killed your lord,   745
forgot the gods and the blood of your glorious brothers.

Listen, listen.
Friends, did you hear a shout? or did anxiety
trick me? a shout deep-rolling like the thunder of Zeus?
Again it comes! The rising wind is charged with news.
Mistress, come out! Electra, leave the house!   750

(Electra appears at the door.)

Electra

Dear friends, what is it? How do we stand now in our trial?

Chorus

I do not know yet—only a voice is crying death.

Electra

I hear it too. It is still faint, far. But I hear it.

Chorus

It comes from a great distance, yet it seems so close.

Electra

It is the Argives groaning there—or is it our friends?   755

Chorus

I cannot tell; the note of clamoring is slurred.

Electra

So you announce my death by sword. Why am I slow?

Chorus

Lady, hold back until you learn the outcome clearly.

Electra

Not possible. We are beaten. Where are the messengers?

Chorus

They will come soon. To kill a king is not quick or light.   760

(Enter a Messenger in excitement.)

Messenger

Hail maidens of Mycenae, beautiful in triumph!
Orestes is victor! I proclaim it to all who love him.
The murderer of Agamemnon lies on the earth
crumpled in blood, Aegisthus. Let us thank the gods.

Electra

Who are you? Why should I think your message is the truth?   765

Messenger

You do not know your brother's servant? You have seen me.

Electra

Dearest of servants! out of fear I held my eyes
shaded from recognition. Now indeed I know you.
What was your news? my father's hated murderer dead?

Messenger

Dead, dead. I will say it twice if that is pleasing.   770

Electra

 O gods! O Justice watching the world, you have come at last.
How did he die? what style of death did Orestes choose,
to kill Thyestes' son? Give me the details.

Messenger

 When we rose from your cottage and walked down the hill
we came across a beaten double wagon-track,   775
and there we found the famous master of Mycenae.
He happened to be walking in the water-meadow,
scything young green shoots of myrtle for his hair.
He saw us and called out: "You are most welcome, strangers.
Who are you? Have you traveled far? Where is your home?"   780
Orestes answered, "We are Thessalians on our way
toward Alpheus' valley where we shall sacrifice to Zeus
of Olympia." When Aegisthus heard, he called again,
"Now you must stop among us as our guests and share
our feast. I am at the moment slaughtering a bull   785
for the Nymphs. Tomorrow morning you shall rise refreshed
and lose no time on the road. Come with me to the shrine—"
while he was still talking he took him by the hand
and led us off the road—"I will take no refusal."
When we had reached his garden hut he gave commands: 790
"Quick, someone fill a bowl of water for the strangers
so their hands will be clean to make lustration at the altar."
But Orestes interrupted: "We are clean enough.
We washed ourselves just now in the clear river water.
If citizens need strangers for your sacrifice   795
we are here, Aegisthus. We shall not refuse you, prince."
 After this they broke off public conversation.
Now the king's bodyguard laid down their spears
and sprang all hands to working.
Some brought the lustral bowl and baskets of holy grain,   800
some laid and lit the fire or around the hearth
set up the sacred ewers—the whole roof rang with sound.
Your mother's lover took the barley in his hands

and cast it on the altar as he said these words:
"Nymphs of the Rocks, I have killed many bulls for you,   805
and my wife, Tyndareus' child, has killed often at home.
Guard us in present fortune, ruin our enemies."
(Meaning you and Orestes.) But my master prayed
the utter reverse, keeping his words below his breath,
to take his dynastic place again. Aegisthus raised   810
the narrow knife from the basket, cut the calf's front lock,
with his right hand dedicated it to the holy fire,
and, as his servants hoisted the beast upon their shoulders,
slashed its throat.

        Now he turns to your brother and says,
"One of your great Thessalian virtues, as you boast,   815
is to be a man of two skills: disjointing bulls
and taming horses. Stranger, take the iron knife,
show us how true Thessalian reputation runs."
Orestes caught the beautifully tempered Dorian blade,
loosened his brooch, flung his fine cloak back from his shoulders,   820
chose Pylades as his assistant in the work,
and made the men stand off. Holding the beast by its foot,
he laid the white flesh bare with one pass of his hand.
He stripped the hide off whole, more quickly than a runner
racing could double down and back the hippodrome course,   825
and loosened the soft belly. Aegisthus scooped the prophetic
viscera up in his hands.

        The liver lobe was not
there. Unhidden, the portal-vein and gall-sac showed
disaster coming at him even as he peered.
His face darkened, drew down. My master watched and asked,   830
"What puts you out of heart?" "Stranger, I am afraid.
Some ambush is at my door. There is a man I hate,
an heir to Agamemnon and his war on my house."
He answered, "You can scarcely fear a fugitive's
tricks when you control the state? Now to appease us   835
with sacrificial flesh, will someone bring a knife—
Phthian, not Dorian—and let me split his breast?"

He took it and struck. Aegisthus heaped the soft parts, then
sorted them out. But while his head was bent above them,
your brother stretched up, balanced on the balls of his feet,   840
and smashed a blow to his spine. The vertebrae of his back
broke. Head down, his whole body convulsed, he gasped
to breathe, writhed with a high scream, and died in his blood.

    The servingmen who saw it flashed straight to their spears,
an army for two men to face. And yet with courage   845
they stood, faced them, shook their javelins, engaged—
both Pylades and Orestes, who cried, "I have not come
in wrath against this city nor against my people.
I have only paid my father's killer back in blood.
I am injured Orestes—do not kill me, men   850
who helped my father's house of old."

                              They, when they heard
his words, lowered their spears, and he was recognized
by some old man who used to serve the family.
Swiftly they crowned your brother's head with flower wreaths,
shouting aloud in joy and triumph. He comes to you   855
bringing a head to show you—not a Gorgon horror,
only Aegisthus whom you loathe, who was in debt
for blood and found the paying bitter at his death.

Chorus

Come, lift your foot, lady, to dance
   now like a fawn who in flying   860
arcs leaps for joy, light, almost brushing the sky.
   He wins a garland of glory
more great than those Alpheus' glades grant to the perfect,
your own brother; now, in the hymn strain,
praise the fair victor, chant to my step.   865

Electra

O flame of day and sun's great chariot charged with light,
O earth below and dark of night where I watched before,
my eyes are clear now, I can unfold my sight to freedom,

now that Aegisthus, who had killed my father, falls.
Bring me my few belongings, what my house keeps treasured   870
as ornaments of splendor for the hair, dear friends,
for I will crown my brother as a conqueror.

Chorus

Lay now the bright signs of success
    over his brow, as we circle
our chorused step, dancing to the Muses' delight.   875
    Now again in our country
our old and loved kings of the blood capture the power,
in high justice routing the unjust.
Raise to the flute's tune shouts of our joy.

                    (Enter Orestes, Pylades, and servants with corpse.)
Electra

O man of triumph sprung of our triumphant father   880
who fought and won below the walls of Troy—Orestes!
Take from my hands these twisted lock-rings for your hair.
You come, a runner in no trifling race, but long
and challenging, to your home goal, killing Aegisthus
who was your enemy, who once destroyed our father.   885
    And you, companion of the shield, Pylades, son
of a most reverend father, please receive your crown
from my hand, for you have won an equal share of glory
in this stark trial. May I see your fortune always high.

Orestes

You must believe, Electra, that the gods have been   890
first founders of our luck; then you may turn to praise
me as the simple servant of both god and luck.
I come to you the killer of Aegisthus, not
in words but action. You know this, but more than this
I have here in my hands the man himself, though dead.   895
You may want to display him for the beasts to eat
or as a toy for carrion birds born of bright air
or stick his head upon a stake. He is all yours.

Electra

I am ashamed to speak and yet I wish to speak.   900

Orestes

What is it? Speak your mind and so emerge from fear.

Electra

I am ashamed to insult the dead; some hate may strike me.

Orestes

There is no man on earth, nor will be, who could blame you.

Electra

Our state is harsh to please and takes delight in slander.

Orestes

Speak as you need to, Sister. We were joined to him   905
in bonds of hatred which could know no gentle truce.

Electra

So be it.
          Which of our sufferings shall I speak in prelude,
which shall I make finale, or marshal in the center?
And yet through rising nights I never once have missed
calling aloud what I wished to tell you to your face   910
if only I were liberated from my fears
of old. We are at the point now. I give you the full
tale of ruin I hoped to tell you in your life.

          You killed me, orphaned me, and him too, of a father
we loved dearly, though he had done no harm to you.   915
In ugliness you bedded my mother, killed her man
who captained the Greeks abroad while you skulked far from
          Phrygia.
You climbed such heights of stupidness that you imagined
your marriage to my mother would not marry you
to cuckoldry, though your own success in Father's bed   920

was criminal. You should know, when a man seduces another's
wife in secret sex and then is forced to keep her,
he heads for disaster if he thinks that she, unchaste
to her first husband, will suddenly turn chaste for him.

Your household life was painful though you could not see it;   925
you knew in your heart that you had made a godless marriage,
and Mother knew she had acquired a godless man,
so each in working pain shouldered the other's load
for mutual help: she got your evil, you got hers.
Every time you walked outdoors in Argos, you heard,   930
"There goes the queen's husband." It was never "the king's wife."

O what perversion, when the woman in the house
stands out as master, not the man. I shake in hate
to see those children whom the city knows and names
not by their father's name but only by their mother's.   935
It marks the bridegroom who has climbed to a nobler bed;
when no one mentions the husband, everyone knows the wife.

Where you were most deceived in your grand unawareness
was your boast to be a man of power since you had money.
Wealth stays with us a little moment if at all;   940
only our characters are steadfast, not our gold,
for character stays with us to the end and faces
trouble, but wealth which lives with us on terms of crime
wings swiftly from the house after brief blossoming.

The women in your life I will not mention—a maiden   945
ought not—but only hint that I know all about them.
You played it haughty since you lived in a grand palace
and were handsome enough. But let me have a husband
not girlish-faced like you but graceful in male courage
whose sons would cling bold to the craggy heights of war;   950
your looks were only ornamental at the dance.

Die then. You paid your debt, never knowing that time
stripped your disguises bare. So should no criminal
who starts his race without a stumble vainly believe
that he has outrun Justice, till in the closing stretch   955
he nears the finish line and gains the goal of death.

Chorus

He wrought horrors, yet has paid in horror to you
and your brother. Justice has enormous power.

Electra

Enough now. Women, take his body out of sight,
conceal it well in darkness so that when she comes   960
my mother sees no corpses till her throat is cut.

(*The corpse is carried into the cottage.*)

Orestes

Hold off a little; we might find another plan.

Electra

What's there? I see some allies racing from Mycenae.

Orestes

Not allies. You are looking at my mother who bore me.

Electra

How beautifully she marches straight into our net;   965
see how grandly she rides with chariot and escort.

Orestes

What—what is our action now toward Mother? Do we kill?

Electra

Don't tell me pity catches you at the sight of her.

Orestes

O god!
How can I kill her when she brought me up and bore me?

Electra

Kill her just the way she killed my father. And yours.   970

Orestes

O Phoebus, your holy word was brute and ignorant.

Electra

Where Apollo is ignorant shall men be wise?

Orestes

He said to kill my mother, whom I must not kill.

Electra

Nothing will hurt you. You are only avenging Father.

Orestes

As matricide I must stand trial. I was clean before.   975

Electra

Not clean before the gods, if you neglect your father.

Orestes

I know—but will I not be judged for killing Mother?

Electra

And will you not be judged for quitting Father's service?

Orestes

A polluted demon spoke it in the shape of god—

Electra

Throned on the holy tripod? I shall not believe you.   980

Orestes

And I shall not believe those oracles were pure.

Electra

You may not play the coward now and fall to weakness.
Go in. I will bait her a trap as she once baited one
which sprang at Aegisthus' touch and killed her lawful husband.

Orestes

I am going in. I walk a cliff-edge in a sea   985
of evil, and evil I will do. If the gods approve,
let it be so. This game of death is bitter, and sweet.

*(Orestes goes slowly into the house with Pylades, without looking back.
Up the road by which he had just come with Aegisthus' corpse, enter Clytemnestra in a chariot, attended by Trojan slave girls.)*

Chorus

    Hail! hail!
Queen and mistress of Argos, hail,
    Tyndareus' child,
sister in blood to the lordly sons   990
of Zeus who dwell in starred and flaming
air, saviors adored by men
    in the roar of the salt sea.
Hail! I honor you like the gods
for your looming wealth and brilliant life.   995
The time to guard and heal your doom
    is now, O Queen. Hail!

Clytemnestra

    Get out of the carriage, Trojan maidens; hold my hand
tight, so I can step down safely to the ground.

                    (Looking around somewhat embarrassed.)
Mostly we gave the houses of our gods the spoils   1000
from Phrygia, but these girls, the best in Troy, I chose
to ornament my own house and replace the child
I lost, my loved daughter. The compensation is small.

Electra

    Then may not I, who am a slave and also tossed
far from my father's home to live in misery,   1005
may I not, Mother, hold your most distinguished hand?

Clytemnestra

    These slaves are here to help me. Do not trouble yourself.

Electra

    Why not? You rooted me up, a casualty of war;
my home was overpowered; I am in your power,
as they are too—left dark, lonely, and fatherless.   1010

Clymnestra

   And dark and lonely were your father's plots against
those he should most have loved and least conspired to kill.
I can tell you—no. When a woman gets an evil
reputation she finds a bitter twist to her words.
This is my case now, not a pretty one. And yet,   1015
if you have something truly to hate, you ought to learn
the facts first; then hate is more decent. But not in the dark.

    My father Tyndareus gave me to your father's care,
not to kill me, not to kill what I bore and loved.
And yet he tempted my daughter, slyly whispering   1020
of marriage with Achilles, took her from home to Aulis
where the ships were stuck, stretched her high above the fire
and, like pale field grass, slashed Iphigenia's throat.
If this had been to save the state from siege and ruin,
if it had helped his home and spared his other children   1025
to rack one girl for many lives, I could have forgiven.
But now for the sake of Helen's lust and for the man
who took a wife and could not punish her seducer—
for their lives' sake he took the life of my dear child.
I was unfairly wronged in this, yet not for this   1030
would I have gone savage so, nor killed my husband so,
but he came home to me with a mad, god-filled girl
and introduced her to our bed. So there we were,
two brides being stabled in a single stall.

    Oh, women are fools for sex, deny it I shall not.   1035
Since this is in our nature, when our husbands choose
to despise the bed they have, a woman is quite willing
to imitate her man and find another friend.
But then the dirty gossip puts us in the spotlight;
the guilty ones, the men, are never blamed at all.   1040
If Menelaus had been raped from home on the sly,
should I have had to kill Orestes so my sister's
husband could be rescued? You think your father would
have borne it? He would have killed me. Then why was it fair
for him to kill what belonged to me and not be killed?   1045

I killed. I turned and walked the only path still open,
straight to his enemies. Would any of his friends
have helped me in the task of murder I had to do?
    Speak if you have need or reason. Fight me free;
demonstrate how your father died without full justice.   1050

Chorus

Justice is in your words but justice can be ugly.
A wife should give way to her husband in all things
if her mind is sound; if she refuses to see this truth
she cannot enter fully counted to my thought.

Electra

Keep in mind, Mother, those last words you spoke,   1055
giving me license to speak out freely against you.

Clytemnestra

I say them once again, child; I will not deny you.

Electra

But when you hear me, Mother, will you hurt me again?

Clytemnestra

Not so at all. I shall be glad to humor you.

Electra

Then I speak—and here is the keynote of my song.   1060
Mother who bore me, how I wish your mind were healthy.
Although for beauty you deserve tremendous praise,
both you and Helen, flowering from a single stalk,
you both grew sly and lightweight, a disgrace to Castor.
When she was raped she walked of her own will to ruin,   1065
while you brought ruin on the finest man in Greece
and screened it with the argument that for your child
you killed your husband. The world knows you less well than I.
    You, long before your daughter came near sacrifice,
the very hour your husband marched away from home,   1070

were setting your brown curls by the bronze mirror's light.
Now any woman who works on her beauty when her man
is gone from home indicts herself as being a whore.
She has no decent cause to show her painted face
outside the door unless she wants to look for trouble.   1075

    Of all Greek women, you were the only one I know
to hug yourself with pleasure when Troy's fortunes rose,
but when they sank, to cloud your face in sympathy.
You needed Agamemnon never to come again.
And yet life gave you every chance to be wise and fine.   1080
You had a husband scarcely feebler than Aegisthus,
whom Greece herself had chosen as her king and captain;
and when your sister Helen—did the things she did,
that was your time to capture glory, for black evil
is outlined clearest to our sight by the blaze of virtue.   1085

    Next. If, as you say, our father killed your daughter,
did I do any harm to you, or did my brother?
When you killed your husband, why did you not bestow
the ancestral home on us, but took to bed the gold
which never belonged to you to buy yourself a lover?   1090
And why has *he* not gone in exile for your son
or died to pay for me who still alive have died
my sister's death twice over while you strangle my life?
If murder judges and calls for murder, I will kill
you—and your own Orestes will kill you—for Father.   1095
If the first death was just, the second too is just.

Clytemnestra

    My child, from birth you always have adored your father.   1102
This is part of life. Some children always love
the male, some turn more closely to their mother than him.
I know you and forgive you. I am not so happy   1105
either, child, with what I have done or with myself.

    How poorly you look. Have you not washed? Your clothes are
      bad.
I suppose you just got up from bed and giving birth?

O god, how miserably my plans have all turned out.
Perhaps I drove my hate too hard against my husband.   1110

Electra

Your mourning comes a little late. There is no cure.
Father is dead now. If you grieve, why not
recall the son you sent to starve in foreign lands?

Clytemnestra

I am afraid. I have to watch my life, not his.
They say his father's death has made him very angry.   1115

Electra

Why do you let your husband act like a beast against us?

Clytemnestra

That is his nature. Yours is wild and stubborn too.

Electra

That hurts. But I am going to bury my anger soon.

Clytemnestra

Good; then he never will be harsh to you again.

Electra

He has been haughty; now he is staying in my house.   1120

Clytemnestra

You see? you want to blow the quarrel to new flames.

Electra

I will be quiet; I fear him—the way I fear him.

Clytemnestra

Stop this talk. You called me here for something, girl.

Electra

I think you heard about my lying-in and son.
Make me the proper sacrifice—I don't know how—   1125

as the law runs for children at the tenth night moon.
I have no knowledge; I never had a family.

Clytemnestra

This is work for the woman who acted as your midwife.

Electra

I acted for myself. I was alone at birth.

Clytemnestra

Your house is set so desolate of friends and neighbors?   1130

Electra

No one is willing to make friends with poverty.

Clytemnestra

Then I will go and make the gods full sacrifice
for a child as law prescribes. I give you so much
grace and then pass to the meadow where my husband rests
praying to the bridal Nymphs. Servants, take the wagon,   1135
set it in the stables. When you think this rite
of god draws to an end, come back to stand beside me,
for I have debts of grace to pay my husband too.

Electra

Enter our poor house. And, Mother, take good care
the smoky walls put no dark stain upon your robes.   1140
Pay sacrifice to heaven as you ought to pay.

> (*Clytemnestra walks alone into the house; the
> Trojan girls withdraw with the chariot.*)

The basket of grain is raised again, the knife is sharp
which killed the bull, and close beside him you shall fall
stricken, to keep your bridal rites in the house of death
with him you slept beside in life. I give you so   1145
much grace and you shall give my father grace of justice.

> (*Electra goes into the cottage.*)

Chorus

Evils are interchanging. The winds of this house
shift now to a new track. Of old in the bath
my captain, mine, fell to his death;
the roof rang, the stone heights of the hall echoed loud   1150
to his cry: "O terrible lady, will you kill me now
newly come home to love at the tenth cycle of seed?"

. . . .

Time circles back and brings her to the bar,   1155
she pays grief for love errant. She, when her lord
came safe home, after dragging years,
where his stone Cyclops' walls rose straight to the sky, there with
      steel
freshly honed to an edge killed him, hand on the ax. O wretched   1160
husband, most wretched suffering must have turned her then:
a lioness mountain-bred, ranging out
from her oak-sheltered home, she sprang. It was done.

Clytemnestra (from inside the house)

O children—O my god—do not kill your mother—no.   1165

Chorus

Do you hear her cry trapped in the walls?

Clytemnestra

O, O, I am hurt—

Chorus

I also am hurt to hear you in your children's hands.
Justice is given down by god soon or late;
you suffer terribly now, you acted terribly then   1170
against god and love.

(*Orestes, Electra, and Pylades emerge from the house, and the
            doors open to reveal the corpses of Aegisthus and
                        Clytemnestra lying together.*)

Behold them coming from the house in robes of blood
newly stained by a murdered mother, walking straight,
living signs of triumph over her frightful cries.
There is no house, nor has there been, more suffering   1175
or more at war than this, the house of Tantalus.

Orestes

O Earth and Zeus who watch all work
men do, look at this work of blood
and corruption, two bodies in death
lying battered along the dirt   1180
under my hands, only to pay
for my pain.

Electra

Weep greatly for me, my brother, I am guilty.
A girl flaming in hurt I marched against
    the mother who bore me.

Chorus

Weep for destiny; destiny yours   1185
to mother unforgettable wrath,
to suffer unforgettable pain
beyond pain at your children's hands.
You paid for their father's death as the law asks.

Orestes

Phoebus, you hymned the law in black   1190
melody, but the deed has shone
white as a scar. You granted us rest
as murderers rest—to leave the land
of Greece. But where else can I go?
What state, host, god-fearing man   1195
will look steady upon my face,
    who killed my mother?

Electra

O weep for me. Where am I now? What dance—
what wedding may I come to? What man will take
   me bride to his bed?   1200

Chorus

Circling, circling, your wilful mind
veers in the blowing wind and turns·
you think piously now, but then
thoughtless you wrought an impious thing,
dear girl, when your brother's will was against you.   1205

Orestes

You saw her agony, how she threw aside her dress,
how she was showing her breast there in the midst of death?
   My god, how she bent to earth
the legs which I was born through? and her hair—I touched it—

Chorus

I know, I understand; you have come   1210
through grinding torment hearing her cry
   so hurt, your own mother.

Orestes

She cracked into a scream then, she stretched up her hand
toward my face: "My son! Oh, be pitiful my son!"   1215
   She clung to my face,
suspended, hanging; my arm dropped with the sword—

Chorus

Unhappy woman—how could your eyes
bear to watch her blood as she fought
   for her breath and died there?   1220

Orestes

I snatched a fold of my cloak to hood my eyes, and, blind,
   took the sword and sacrificed
my mother—sank steel to her neck.

Electra

    I urged you on, I urged you on,
    I touched the sword beside your hand.   1225

Chorus

    Working a terrible pain and ruin.

Orestes

    Take it! shroud my mother's dead flesh in my cloak,
       clean and close the sucking wounds.
    You carried your own death in your womb.

Electra

    Behold! I wrap her close in the robe,   1230
    the one I loved and could not love.

Chorus

    Ending your family's great disasters.

    (The Dioscuri appear on the roof over the scene of mourning.)

    Whom do I see high over your house
    shining in radiance? Are they divinities
    or gods of the heavens? They are more than men   1235
    in their moving. Why do they come so bright
       into the eyes of mortals?

                Dioscuri (Castor speaking for both.)

    O son of Agamemnon, hear us: we call to you,
    the Twins, born with your mother, named the sons of Zeus,
    I Castor, and my brother Polydeuces here.   1240
    We come to Argos having turned the rolling storm
    of a sea-tossed ship to quiet, when we saw the death
    of this our murdered sister, of your murdered mother.
    Justice has claimed her but you have not worked in justice.
    As for Phoebus, Phoebus—yet he is my lord,   1245
    silence. He knows the truth but his oracles were lies.

Compulsion is on us to accept this scene, on you
to go complete the doom which fate and Zeus decreed.
    Give Pylades Electra as a wife in his house,
and leave Argos yourself. The city is not yours   1250
to walk in any longer, since you killed your mother.
The dreadful beast-faced goddesses of destiny
will roll you like a wheel through maddened wandering.
But when you come to Athens, fold the holy wood
of Pallas' statue to your breast—then she will check   1255
the fluttering horror of their snakes, they cannot touch you
as she holds her Gorgon-circled shield above your head.
    In Athens is the Hill of Ares, where the gods
first took their seats to judge murder by public vote,
the time raw-minded Ares killed Halirrhothius   1260
in anger at his daughter's godless wedding night,
in anger at the sea-lord's son. Since then this court
has been holy and trusted by both men and gods.
There you also must run the risk of trial for murder.
But the voting-pebbles will be cast equal and save you,   1265
you shall not die by the verdict: Loxias will take
all blame on himself for having asked your mother's death,
and so for the rest of time this law shall be established:
When votes are equal the accused must have acquittal.
The dreadful goddesses, shaken in grief for this,   1270
shall go down in a crack of earth beside the Hill
to keep a dark and august oracle for men.
Then you must found a city near Arcadian
Alpheus' stream, beside the wolf-god's sanctuary,
and by your name that city shall be known to men.   1275
    So much I say to you. Aegisthus' corpse the men
of Argos will hide, buried in an earth-heaped tomb.
Menelaus will bury your mother. He has come just now
to Nauplia for the first time since he captured Troy.
Helen will help him. She is home from Proteus' halls,   1280
leaving Egypt astern. She never went to Troy.
Zeus fashioned and dispatched a Helen-image there

to Ilium so men might die in hate and blood.
So. Let Pylades take Electra, girl and wife,
and start his journey homeward, leaving Achaea's lands;   1285
let him also to his Phocian estates escort
your "brother," as they call him—set him deep in wealth.
Turn your feet toward Isthmus' narrow neck of earth,
make your way to the blessed hill where Cecrops dwells.
When you have drained the fulness of a murderer's doom   1290
you may again be happy, released from these distresses.

Chorus

Sons of Zeus, does the law allow us
to draw any closer toward your voice?

Dioscuri

The law allows, you are clean of this blood.

Electra

Will you speak to me too, Tyndaridae?   1295

Dioscuri

Also to you. On Phoebus I place all
    guilt for this death.

Chorus

Why could you, who are gods and brothers
    of the dead woman here,
not turn her Furies away from our halls?   1300

Dioscuri

Doom is compelling, it leads and we follow—
doom and the brutal song of Apollo.

Electra

And I? What Apollo, what oracle's voice
ordained I be marked in my mother's blood?

Dioscuri

    You shared in the act, you share in the fate: 1305
      both children a single
  curse on your house has ground into dust.

Orestes

    O Sister, I found you so late, and so soon
    I lose you, robbed of your healing love,
    and leave you behind as you have left me.   1310

Dioscuri

    She has a husband, she has a home, she
    needs no pity, she suffers nothing
      but exile from Argos.

Electra

    Are there more poignant sorrows or greater
    than leaving the soil of a fatherland?   1315

Orestes

    But I go too, I am forced from my father's
    home, I must suffer foreigners' judgment
    for the blood of my mother.

Dioscuri

                Courage. You go
    to the holy city of Pallas. Endure.   1320

Electra

    Hold me now closely breast against breast,
      dear Brother. I love you.
    But the curses bred in a mother's blood
    dissolve our bonds and drive us from home.

Orestes

    Come to me, clasp my body, lament   1325
    as if at the tomb of a man now dead.

Dioscuri

    Alas, your despair rings terribly, even
        to listening gods;
    pity at mortal labor and pain still
    lives in us and the lords of heaven.   1330

Orestes

    I shall not see you again.

Electra

    I shall never more walk in the light of your eye.

Orestes

    Now is the last I can hear your voice.

Electra

    Farewell, my city.
    Many times farewell, fellow citizens.   1335

Orestes

    O loyal love, do you go so soon?

Electra

    I go. These tears are harsh for my eyes.

Orestes

    Pylades, go, farewell; and be kind to   1340
        Electra in marriage.

Dioscuri

    Marriage shall fill their minds. But the hounds
    are here. Quick, to Athens! Run to escape,
    for they hurl their ghostly tracking against you,
    serpent-fisted and blackened of flesh,   1345
    offering the fruit of terrible pain.
    We two must rush to Sicilian seas,
    rescue the salt-smashed prows of the fleet.

As we move through the open valleys of air
we champion none who are stained in sin,   1350
but those who have held the holy and just
dear in their lives we will loose from harsh
   sorrow and save them.
So let no man be desirous of evil
nor sail with those who have broken their oaths—   1355
   as god to man I command you.

Chorus

Farewell. The mortal who can fare well,
not broken by trouble met on the road,
   leads a most blessèd life.

THE TROJAN WOMEN[1]

Translated by Richmond Lattimore

1. This translation first appeared in *Greek Plays in Modern Translation,*
edited with an Introduction by Dudley Fitts (Copyright, Dial Press, 1947).
It is used here by kind permission of The Dial Press, Inc. Some alterations
have been made, chiefly in the matter of spelling Greek names.

INTRODUCTION

The Trojan Women was part of a connected "trilogy" dealing with the general subject of the Trojan War. It was preceded by *Alexander* and *Palamedes* and followed by the satyr-play *Sisyphus*. These plays are lost. The trilogy was presented in 415 B.C. and won the second prize.

There can be no doubt that in this play Euripides used heroic legend for the expression of his feelings about the horrors of aggressive war in his own time. In 416, Athens had tried to force the neutral island state of Melos to join the Athenian confederacy. This was in peacetime. The Melians were besieged and blockaded. They capitulated, and all grown male citizens were put to death, and their women and children were enslaved. This was, however, only the most recent and most flagrant of the abuses of power shown by both sides during hostilities dating back to 431 B.C. Moreover, the Athenians at the time of the trilogy were about to launch their great (unprovoked) expedition to conquer Sicily. But Euripides is not, I think, specifically against Athens. He is against all warmakers.

The action of *The Trojan Women* occupies the time between the fall of Troy and the departure of the Greek fleet for home—a fleet, so the prologue tells us, which will be wrecked with much loss. At the opening, all the Trojan men are dead or vanished. The women are dealt out to their future masters. The child Astyanax, son of Hector, is slaughtered "as a measure of safety." Finally, the greatest of the "Trojan Women," Troy herself, is annihilated. There is no dramatic solution, no relief. The innocent suffer. Odysseus, the villain behind the scenes, triumphs, and, of the persons who appear, only the stuffy, weak-willed Spartan Menelaus and Helen, his pretty, clever, faithless, worthless Spartan wife, come out safe and sound. For, despite the predictions of wreck and hardship, all readers of *The Odyssey* knew that Helen, Menelaus, and Odysseus survived to a prosperous old age.

CHARACTERS

Poseidon

Athene

Hecuba

Talthybius

Cassandra

Andromache

Astyanax

Menelaus

Helen

Chorus of Trojan women

THE TROJAN WOMEN

SCENE: *The action takes place shortly after the capture of Troy. All Trojan men have been killed, or have fled; all women and children are captives. The scene is an open space before the city, which is visible in the background, partly demolished and smoldering. Against the walls are tents, or huts, which temporarily house the captive women. The entrance of the Chorus is made, in two separate groups which subsequently unite, from these buildings, as are those of Cassandra and Helen. The entrances of Talthybius, Andromache, and Menelaus are made from the wings. It is imaginable that the gods are made to appear high up, above the level of the other actors, as if near their own temples on the Citadel. As the play opens, Hecuba is prostrate on the ground (it is understood that she hears nothing of what the gods say).*

(*Enter Poseidon.*)

Poseidon

I am Poseidon. I come from the Aegean depths
of the sea beneath whose waters Nereid choirs evolve
the intricate bright circle of their dancing feet.
For since that day when Phoebus Apollo and I laid down
on Trojan soil the close of these stone walls, drawn true   5
and straight, there has always been affection in my heart
unfading, for these Phrygians and for their city;
which smolders now, fallen before the Argive spears,
ruined, sacked, gutted. Such is Athene's work, and his,
the Parnassian, Epeius of Phocis, architect   10
and builder of the horse that swarmed with inward steel,
that fatal bulk which passed within the battlements,
whose fame hereafter shall be loud among men unborn,
the Wooden Horse, which hid the secret spears within.
Now the gods' groves are desolate, their thrones of power   15
blood-spattered where beside the lift of the altar steps
of Zeus Defender, Priam was cut down and died.

The ships of the Achaeans load with spoils of Troy
now, the piled gold of Phrygia. And the men of Greece
who made this expedition and took the city, stay   20
only for the favoring stern-wind now to greet their wives
and children after ten years' harvests wasted here.

The will of Argive Hera and Athene won
its way against my will. Between them they broke Troy.
So I must leave my altars and great Ilium,   25
since once a city sinks into sad desolation
the gods' state sickens also, and their worship fades.
Scamander's valley echoes to the wail of slaves,
the captive women given to their masters now,
some to Arcadia or the men of Thessaly   30
assigned, or to the lords of Athens, Theseus' strain;
while all the women of Troy yet unassigned are here
beneath the shelter of these walls, chosen to wait
the will of princes, and among them Tyndareus' child
Helen of Sparta, named—with right—a captive slave.   35

Nearby, beside the gates, for any to look upon
who has the heart, she lies face upward, Hecuba
weeping for multitudes her multitude of tears.
Polyxena, one daughter, even now was killed
in secrecy and pain beside Achilles' tomb.   40
Priam is gone, their children dead; one girl is left,
Cassandra, reeling crazed at King Apollo's stroke,
whom Agamemnon, in despite of the gods' will
and all religion, will lead by force to his secret bed.

O city, long ago a happy place, good-bye;   45
good-bye, hewn bastions. Pallas, child of Zeus, did this.
But for her hatred, you might stand strong-founded still.

                                                    (*Athene enters.*)
Athene
    August among the gods, O vast divinity,
    closest in kinship to the father of all, may one
    who quarreled with you in the past make peace, and speak?   50

Poseidon

You may, lady Athene; for the strands of kinship
close drawn work no weak magic to enchant the mind.

Athene

I thank you for your gentleness, and bring you now
questions whose issue touches you and me, my lord.

Poseidon

Is this the annunciation of some new word spoken   55
by Zeus, or any other of the divinities?

Athene

No; but for Troy's sake, on whose ground we stand, I come
to win the favor of your power, and an ally.

Poseidon

You hated Troy once; did you throw your hate away
and change to pity now its walls are black with fire?   60

Athene

Come back to the question. Will you take counsel with me
and help me gladly in all that I would bring to pass?

Poseidon

I will indeed; but tell me what you wish to do.
Are you here for the Achaeans' or the Phrygians' sake?

Athene

For the Trojans, whom I hated this short time since,   65
to make the Achaeans' homecoming a thing of sorrow.

Poseidon

This is a springing change of sympathy. Why must
you hate too hard, and love too hard, your loves and hates?

Athene

Did you not know they outraged my temple, and shamed me?

Poseidon

I know that Ajax dragged Cassandra there by force.   70

Athene

And the Achaeans did nothing. They did not even speak.

Poseidon

    Yet Ilium was taken by your strength alone.

Athene

    True; therefore help me. I would do some evil to them.

Poseidon

    I am ready for anything you ask. What will you do?

Athene

    Make the home voyage a most unhappy coming home.   75

Poseidon

    While they stay here ashore, or out on the deep sea?

Athene

    When they take ship from Ilium and set sail for home
    Zeus will shower down his rainstorms and the weariless beat
    of hail, to make black the bright air with roaring winds.
    He has promised my hand the gift of the blazing thunderbolt   80
    to dash and overwhelm with fire the Achaean ships.
    Yours is your own domain, the Aegaean crossing. Make
    the sea thunder to the tripled wave and spinning surf,
    cram thick the hollow Euboean fold with floating dead;
    so after this Greeks may learn how to use with fear   85
    my sacred places, and respect all gods beside.

Poseidon

    This shall be done, and joyfully. It needs no long
    discourse to tell you. I will shake the Aegaean Sea.
    Myconos' nesses and the swine-back reefs of Delos,
    the Capherean promontories, Scyros, Lemnos   90
    shall take the washed up bodies of men drowned at sea.
    Back to Olympus now, gather the thunderbolts
    from your father's hands, then take your watcher's post, to wait
    the chance, when the Achaean fleet puts out to sea.

    That mortal who sacks fallen cities is a fool,   95
    who gives the temples and the tombs, the hallowed places
    of the dead to desolation. His own turn must come.

*(The gods leave the stage. Hecuba seems to waken, and
gets slowly to her feet as she speaks.)*

Hecuba

Rise, stricken head, from the dust;
lift up the throat. This is Troy, but Troy
and we, Troy's kings, are perished.   100
Stoop to the changing fortune.
Steer for the crossing and the death-god,
hold not life's prow on the course against
wave beat and accident.
Ah me,   105
what need I further for tears' occasion,
state perished, my sons, and my husband?
O massive pride that my fathers heaped
to magnificence, you meant nothing.
Must I be hushed? Were it better thus?   110
Should I cry a lament?
Unhappy, accursed,
limbs cramped, I lie
backed on earth's stiff bed.
O head, O temples   115
and sides; sweet, to shift,
let the tired spine rest
weight eased by the sides alternate,
against the strain of the tears' song
where the stricken people find music yet   120
in the song undanced of their wretchedness.

You ships' prows, that the fugitive
oars swept back to blessed Ilium
over the sea's blue water
by the placid harbors of Hellas   125
to the flute's grim beat
and the swing of the shrill boat whistles;
you made the crossing, made fast ashore
the Egyptians' skill, the sea cables,
alas, by the coasts of Troy;   130

it was you, ships, that carried the fatal bride
of Menelaus, Castor her brother's shame,
the stain on the Eurotas.
Now she has killed
the sire of the fifty sons,   135
Priam; me, unhappy Hecuba,
she drove on this reef of ruin.

Such state I keep
to sit by the tents of Agamemnon.
I am led captive   140
from my house, an old, unhappy woman,
like my city ruined and pitiful.
Come then, sad wives of the Trojans
whose spears were bronze,
their daughters, brides of disaster,
let us mourn the smoke of Ilium.   145
And I, as among winged birds
the mother, lead out
the clashing cry, the song; not that song
wherein once long ago,
when I held the scepter of Priam,   150
my feet were queens of the choir and led
the proud dance to the gods of Phrygia.

> (*The First Half-chorus comes out of the shelter*
> *at the back.*)

First Half-chorus
  Hecuba, what are these cries?
  What news now? For through the walls
  I heard your pitiful weeping.   155
  and fear shivered in the breasts
  of the Trojan women, who within
  sob out the day of their slavery.

Hecuba
  My children, the ships of the Argives
  will move today. The hand is at the oar.   160

First Half-chorus
    They will? Why? Must I take ship
    so soon from the land of my fathers?

Hecuba
    I know nothing. I look for disaster.

First Half-chorus
    Alas!
    Poor women of Troy, torn from your homes,   165
    bent to forced hard work.
    The Argives push for home.

Hecuba
    Oh,
    let her not come forth,
    not now, my child
    Cassandra, driven delirious   170
    to shame us before the Argives;
    not the mad one, to bring fresh pain to my pain.
    Ah no.
    Troy, ill-starred Troy, this is the end;
    your last sad people leave you now,   175
    still alive, and broken.

                  (The Second Half-chorus comes out of the shelter
                                          at the back.)

Second Half-chorus
    Ah me. Shivering, I left the tents
    of Agamemnon to listen.
    Tell us, our queen. Did the Argive council
    decree our death?
    Or are the seamen manning the ships now,   180
    oars ready for action?

Hecuba
    My child, do not fear so. Lighten your heart.
    But I go stunned with terror.

Second Half-chorus
    Has a herald come from the Danaans yet?
    Whose wretched slave shall I be ordained?   185

Hecuba
    You are near the lot now.

Second Half-chorus
    Alas!
    Who will lead me away? An Argive?
    To an island home? To Phthiotis?
    Unhappy, surely, and far from Troy.

Hecuba
    And I,   190
    whose wretched slave
    shall I be? Where, in my gray age,
    a faint drone,
    poor image of a corpse,
    weak shining among dead men? Shall
    I stand and keep guard at their doors,
    shall I nurse their children, I who in Troy   195
    held state as a princess?

*(The two half-choruses now unite to form a
single Chorus.)*

Chorus
    So pitiful, so pitiful
    your shame and your lamentation.
    No longer shall I move the shifting pace
    of the shuttle at the looms of Ida.   200
    I shall look no more on the bodies of my sons.
    No more. Shall I be a drudge besides
    or be forced to the bed of Greek masters?
    Night is a queen, but I curse her.
    Must I draw the water of Pirene,   205
    a servant at sacred springs?
    Might I only be taken to Athens, domain
    of Theseus, the bright, the blessed!

Never to the whirl of Eurotas, not Sparta   210
detested, who gave us Helen,
not look with slave's eyes on the scourge
of Troy, Menelaus.

I have heard the rumor
of the hallowed ground by Peneus,   215
bright doorstone of Olympus,
deep burdened in beauty of flower and harvest.
There would I be next after the blessed,
the sacrosanct hold of Theseus.
And they say that the land of Aetna,   220
the Fire God's keep against Punic men,
mother of Sicilian mountains, sounds
in the herald's cry for games' garlands;
and the land washed
by the streaming Ionian Sea,   225
that land watered by the loveliest
of rivers, Crathis, with the red-gold tresses
who draws from the depths of enchanted wells
blessings on a strong people.

See now, from the host of the Danaans   230
the herald, charged with new orders, takes
the speed of his way toward us.
What message? What command? Since we count as slaves
even now in the Dorian kingdom.

> (*Talthybius enters, followed by a detail of
> armed soldiers.*)

Talthybius
　　Hecuba, incessantly my ways have led me to Troy   235
　　as the messenger of all the Achaean armament.
　　You know me from the old days, my lady; I am sent,
　　Talthybius, with new messages for you to hear.

Hecuba
　　It comes, beloved daughters of Troy; the thing I feared.

Talthybius

You are all given your masters now. Was this your dread?   240

Hecuba

Ah, yes. Is it Phthia, then? A city of Thessaly?
Tell me. The land of Cadmus?

Talthybius

All are allotted separately, each to a man.

Hecuba

Who is given to whom? Oh, is there any hope
left for the women of Troy?   245

Talthybius

I understand. Yet ask not for all, but for each apart.

Hecuba

Who was given my child? Tell me, who shall be lord
of my poor abused Cassandra?

Talthybius

King Agamemnon chose her. She was given to him.

Hecuba

Slave woman to that Lacedaemonian wife?
My unhappy child!   250

Talthybius

No. Rather to be joined with him in the dark bed of love.

Hecuba

She, Apollo's virgin, blessed in the privilege
the gold-haired god gave her, a life forever unwed?

Talthybius

Love's archery and the prophetic maiden struck him hard.   255

Hecuba

Dash down, my daughter,
the keys of your consecration,
break the god's garlands to your throat gathered.

Talthybius

Is it not high favor to be brought to a king's bed?

Hecuba

My poor youngest, why did you take her away from me?   260

Talthybius

You spoke now of Polyxena. Is it not so?

Hecuba

To whose arms did the lot force her?

Talthybius

She is given a guardianship, to keep Achilles' tomb.

Hecuba

To watch, my child? Over a tomb?   265
Tell me, is this their way,
some law, friend, established among the Greeks?

Talthybius

Speak of your child in words of blessing. She feels no pain.

Hecuba

What did that mean? Does she live in the sunlight still?

Talthybius

She lives her destiny, and her cares are over now.   270

Hecuba

The wife of bronze-embattled Hector: tell me of her,
Andromache the forlorn. What shall she suffer now?

Talthybius

The son of Achilles chose her. She was given to him.

Hecuba

And I, my aged strength crutched for support on staves,   275
whom shall I serve?

Talthybius

You shall be slave to Odysseus, lord of Ithaca.

Hecuba

Oh no, no!
Tear the shorn head,
rip nails through the folded cheeks.   280

Must I?
To be given as slave to serve that vile, that slippery man,
right's enemy, brute, murderous beast,
that mouth of lies and treachery, that makes void   285
faith in things promised
and that which was beloved turns to hate. Oh, mourn,
daughters of Ilium, weep as one for me.
I am gone, doomed, undone,
O wretched, given   290
the worst lot of all.

Chorus

I know your destiny now, Queen Hecuba. But mine?
What Hellene, what Achaean is my master now?

Talthybius

Men-at-arms, do your duty. Bring Cassandra forth
without delay. Our orders are to deliver her   295
to the general at once. And afterwards we can bring
to the rest of the princes their allotted captive women.
But see! What is that burst of a torch flame inside?
What can it mean? Are the Trojan women setting fire
to their chambers, at point of being torn from their land   300
to sail for Argos? Have they set themselves aflame
in longing for death? I know it is the way of freedom
in times like these to stiffen the neck against disaster.
Open, there, open; let not the fate desired by these,
dreaded by the Achaeans, hurl their wrath on me.   305

Hecuba

You are wrong, there is no fire there. It is my Cassandra
whirled out on running feet in the passion of her frenzy.

> (*Cassandra, carrying a flaming torch, bursts
> from the shelter.*)

Cassandra

Lift up, heave up; carry the flame; I bring fire of worship,
torches to the temple.
Io, Hymen, my lord. Hymenaeus.   310

Blessed the bridegroom.
Blessed am I indeed to lie at a king's side,
blessed the bride of Argos.
Hymen, my lord, Hymenaeus.
Yours were the tears, my mother,   315
yours was the lamentation for my father fallen,
for your city so dear beloved,
but mine this marriage, my marriage,
and I shake out the torch-flare,   320
brightness, dazzle,
light for you, Hymenaeus,
Hecate, light for you,
for the bed of virginity as man's custom ordains.

Let your feet dance, rippling the air; let go the chorus,   325
as when my father's
fate went in blessedness.
O sacred circle of dance.
Lead now, Phoebos Apollo; I wear your laurel,
I tend your temple,   330
Hymen, O Hymenaeus.
Dance, Mother, dance, laugh; lead; let your feet
wind in the shifting pattern and follow mine,
keep the sweet step with me,
cry out the name Hymenaeus   335
and the bride's name in the shrill
and the blessed incantation.
O you daughters of Phrygia robed in splendor,
dance for my wedding,
for the lord fate appointed to lie beside me.   340

Chorus
Can you not, Queen Hecuba, stop this bacchanal before
her light feet whirl her away into the Argive camp?

Hecuba
Fire God, in mortal marriages you lift up your torch,
but here you throw a melancholy light, not seen

through my hopes that went so high in days gone past. O
    child,   345
there was a time I dreamed you would not wed like this,
not at the spear's edge, not under force of Argive arms.
Let me take the light; crazed, passionate, you cannot carry
it straight enough, poor child. Your fate is intemperate
as you are, always. There is no relief for you.   350

           (*Attendants come from the shelter. Hecuba gently takes the*
                              torch from Cassandra and gives
                                  it to them to carry away.)

You Trojan women, take the torch inside, and change
to songs of tears this poor girl's marriage melodies.

Cassandra

    O Mother, star my hair with flowers of victory.
I know you would not have it happen thus; and yet
this is a king I marry; then be glad; escort   355
the bride. Oh, thrust her strongly on. If Loxias
is Loxias still, the Achaeans' pride, great Agamemnon
has won a wife more fatal than ever Helen was.
Since I will kill him; and avenge my brothers' blood
and my father's in the desolation of his house.   360
But I leave this in silence and sing not now the ax
to drop against my throat and other throats than mine,
the agony of the mother murdered, brought to pass
from our marriage rites, and Atreus' house made desolate.
I am ridden by God's curse still, yet I will step so far   365
out of my frenzy as to show this city's fate
is blessed beside the Achaeans'. For one woman's sake,
one act of love, these hunted Helen down and threw
thousands of lives away. Their general—clever man—
in the name of a vile woman cut his darling down,   370
gave up for a brother the sweetness of children in his house,
all to bring back that brother's wife, a woman who went
of her free will, not caught in constraint of violence.
The Achaeans came beside Scamander's banks, and died

day after day, though none sought to wrench their land from
    them   375
nor their own towering cities. Those the War God caught
never saw their sons again, nor were they laid to rest
decently in winding sheets by their wives' hands, but lie
buried in alien ground; while all went wrong at home
as the widows perished, and barren couples raised and nursed   380
the children of others, no survivor left to tend
the tombs, and what is left there, with blood sacrificed.
For such success as this congratulate the Greeks.
No, but the shame is better left in silence, for fear
my singing voice become the voice of wretchedness.   385
The Trojans have that glory which is loveliest:
they died for their own country. So the bodies of all
who took the spears were carried home in loving hands,
brought, in the land of their fathers, to the embrace of earth
and buried becomingly as the rite fell due. The rest,   390
those Phrygians who escaped death in battle, day by day
came home to happiness the Achaeans could not know;
their wives, their children. Then was Hector's fate so sad?
You think so. Listen to the truth. He is dead and gone
surely, but with reputation, as a valiant man.   395
How could this be, except for the Achaeans' coming?
Had they held back, none might have known how great he
    was.
The bride of Paris was the daughter of Zeus. Had he
not married her, fame in our house would sleep in silence still.
Though surely the wise man will forever shrink from war,   400
yet if war come, the hero's death will lay a wreath
not lustreless on the city. The coward alone brings shame.
Let no more tears fall, Mother, for our land, nor for
this marriage I make; it is by marriage that I bring
to destruction those whom you and I have hated most.   405

Chorus
    You smile on your disasters. Can it be that you
    some day will illuminate the darkness of this song?

Talthybius

    Were it not Apollo who has driven wild your wits
    I would make you sorry for sending the princes of our host
    on their way home in augury of foul speech like this.   410
    Now pride of majesty and wisdom's outward show
    have fallen to stature less than what was nothing worth
    since he, almighty prince of the assembled Hellenes,
    Atreus' son beloved, has stooped—by his own will—
    to find his love in a crazed girl. I, a plain man,   415
    would not marry this woman or keep her as my slave.
    You then, with your wits unhinged by idiocy,
    your scolding of Argos and your Trojans glorified
    I throw to the winds to scatter them. Come now with me
    to the ships, a bride—and such a bride—for Agamemnon.   420

    Hecuba, when Laertes' son calls you, be sure
    you follow; if what all say who came to Ilium
    is true, at the worst you will be a good woman's slave.

Cassandra

    That servant is a vile thing. Oh, how can heralds keep
    their name of honor? Lackeys for despots be they, or   425
    lackeys to the people, all men must despise them still.
    You tell me that my mother must be slave in the house
    of Odysseus? Where are all Apollo's promises
    uttered to me, to my own ears, that Hecuba
    should die in Troy? Odysseus I will curse no more,   430
    poor wretch, who little dreams of what he must go through
    when he will think Troy's pain and mine were golden grace
    beside his own luck. Ten years he spent here, and ten
    more years will follow before he at last comes home, forlorn
    after the terror of the rock and the thin strait,   435
    Charybdis; and the mountain striding Cyclops, who eats
    men's flesh; the Ligyan witch who changes men to swine,
    Circe; the wreck of all his ships on the salt sea,
    the lotus passion, the sacred oxen of the Sun

slaughtered, and dead flesh moaning into speech, to make   440
Odysseus listening shiver. Cut the story short:
he will go down to the water of death, and return alive
to reach home and the thousand sorrows waiting there.

Why must I transfix each of Odysseus' labors one by one?
Lead the way quick to the house of death where I shall
    take my mate.   445
Lord of all the sons of Danaus, haughty in your mind of pride,
not by day, but evil in the evil night you shall find your grave
when I lie corpse-cold and naked next my husband's sepulcher,
piled in the ditch for animals to rip and feed on, beaten by
streaming storms of winter, I who wore Apollo's sacraments.   450
Garlands of the god I loved so well, the spirit's dress of pride,
leave me, as I leave those festivals where once I was so gay.
See, I tear your adornments from my skin not yet defiled by
    touch,
throw them to the running winds to scatter, O lord of prophecy,
Where is this general's ship, then? Lead me where I must set my
    feet on board.   455
Wait the wind of favor in the sails; yet when the ship goes out
from this shore, she carries one of the three Furies in my shape.
Land of my ancestors, good-bye; O Mother, weep no more for
    me.
You beneath the ground, my brothers, Priam, father of us all,
I will be with you soon and come triumphant to the dead below,   460
leaving behind me, wrecked, the house of Atreus, which de-
    stroyed our house.

            (*Cassandra is taken away by Talthybius and his soldiers.
                                            Hecuba collapses.*)
Chorus
    Handmaids of aged Hecuba, can you not see
    how your mistress, powerless to cry out, lies prone? Oh, take
    her hand and help her to her feet, you wretched maids.
    Will you let an aged helpless woman lie so long?   465

Hecuba

No. Let me lie where I have fallen. Kind acts, my maids,
must be unkind, unwanted. All that I endure
and have endured and shall, deserves to strike me down.
O gods! What wretched things to call on—gods!—for help
although the decorous action is to invoke their aid   470
when all our hands lay hold on is unhappiness.
No. It is my pleasure first to tell good fortune's tale,
to cast its count more sadly against disasters now.
I was a princess, who was once a prince's bride,
mother by him of sons pre-eminent, beyond   475
the mere numbers of them, lords of the Phrygian domain,
such sons for pride to point to as no woman of Troy,
no Hellene, none in the outlander's wide world might match.
And then I saw them fall before the spears of Greece,
and cut this hair for them, and laid it on their graves.   480
I mourned their father, Priam. None told me the tale
of his death. I saw it, with these eyes. I stood to watch
his throat cut, next the altar of the protecting god.
I saw my city taken. And the girls I nursed,
choice flowers to wear the pride of any husband's eyes,   485
matured to be dragged by hands of strangers from my arms.
There is no hope left that they will ever see me more,
no hope that I shall ever look on them again.
There is one more stone to key this arch of wretchedness:
I must be carried away to Hellas now, an old   490
slave woman, where all those tasks that wrack old age shall be
given me by my masters. I must work the bolt
that bars their doorway, I whose son was Hector once;
or bake their bread; lay down these withered limbs to sleep
on the bare ground, whose bed was royal once; abuse   495
this skin once delicate the slattern's way, exposed
through robes whose rags will mock my luxury of long since.
Unhappy, O unhappy. And all this came to pass
and shall be, for the way one woman chose a man.
Cassandra, O Daughter, whose excitements were the god's,   500

you have paid for your consecration now; at what a price!
And you, my poor Polyxena, where are you now?
Not here, nor any boy or girl of mine, who were
so many once, is near me in my unhappiness.
And you would lift me from the ground? What hope? What use?   505
Guide these feet long ago so delicate in Troy,
a slave's feet now, to the straw sacks laid on the ground
and the piled stones; let me lay down my head and die
in an exhaustion of tears. Of all who walk in bliss
call not one happy yet, until the man is dead.   510

> *(Hecuba, after being led to the back of the stage, flings herself*
> *to the ground once more.)*

Chorus
 Voice of singing, stay
 with me now, for Ilium's sake;
 take up the burden of tears,
 the song of sorrow;
 the dirge for Troy's death   515
 must be chanted;
 the tale of my captivity
 by the wheeled stride of the four-foot beast of the Argives,
 the horse they left in the gates,
 thin gold at its brows,   520
 inward, the spears' high thunder.
 Our people thronging
 the rock of Troy let go the great cry:
 "The war is over! Go down,
 bring back the idol's enchanted wood   525
 to the Maiden of Ilium, Zeus' daughter."
 Who stayed then? Not one girl, not one
 old man, in their houses,
 but singing for happiness
 let the lurking death in.   530

 And the generation of Troy
 swept solid to the gates

to give the goddess
her pleasure: the colt immortal, unbroken,
the nest of Argive spears,
death for the children of Dardanus   535
sealed in the sleek hill pine chamber.
In the sling of the flax twist shipwise
they berthed the black hull
in the house of Pallas Athene   540
stone paved, washed now in the blood of our people.
Strong, gay work
deep into black night
to the stroke of the Libyan lute
and all Troy singing, and girls'   545
light feet pulsing the air
in the kind dance measures;
indoors, lights everywhere,
torchflares on black
to forbid sleep's onset.   550

I was there also: in the great room
I danced the maiden of the mountains,
Artemis, Zeus' daughter.
When the cry went up, sudden,   555
bloodshot, up and down the city, to stun
the keep of the citadel. Children
reached shivering hands to clutch
at the mother's dress.
War stalked from his hiding place.   560
Pallas did this.
Beside their altars the Trojans
died in their blood. Desolate now,
men murdered, our sleeping rooms gave up
their brides' beauty   565
to breed sons for Greek men,
sorrow for our own country.

*(A wagon comes on the stage. It is heaped with a number of
spoils of war, in the midst of which sits Andromache
holding Astyanax. While the chorus continues
speaking, Hecuba rises once more.)*

Hecuba look, I see her, rapt
to the alien wagon, Andromache,
close to whose beating breast clings   570
the boy Astyanax, Hector's sweet child.
O carried away—to what land?—unhappy woman,
on the wagon floor, with the brazen arms
of Hector, of Troy
captive and heaped beside you,
torn now from Troy, for Achilles' son   575
to hang in the shrines of Phthia.

Andromache
I am in the hands of Greek masters.

Hecuba
Alas!

Andromache
    Must the incantation

Hecuba
(ah me!)

Andromache
    of my own grief win tears from you?

Hecuba
It must—O Zeus!

Andromache
      My own distress?   580

Hecuba
O my children

Andromache
    once. No longer.

Hecuba
Lost, lost, Troy our dominion

Andromache
  unhappy

Hecuba
        and my lordly children.

Andromache
  Gone, alas!

Hecuba
          They were mine.

Andromache
  Sorrows only.

Hecuba
                Sad destiny   585

Andromache
  of our city

Hecuba
          a wreck, and burning.

Andromache
  Come back, O my husband.

Hecuba
  Poor child, you invoke
  a dead man; my son once

Andromache
  my defender.   590

Hecuba
  And you, whose death shamed the Achaeans,

Andromache
  lord of us all once,
  O patriarch, Priam,

Hecuba
  take me to my death now.

Andromache
  Longing for death drives deep;

Hecuba

                      O sorrowful, such is our fortune;   595

Andromache
  lost our city

Hecuba

            and our pain lies deep under pain piled over.

Andromache
  We are the hated of God, since once your youngest escaping
  death, brought down Troy's towers in the arms of a worthless
      woman,
  piling at the feet of Pallas the bleeding bodies of our young men
  sprawled, kites' food, while Troy takes up the yoke of captivity.   600

Hecuba
  O my city, my city forlorn

Andromache

                abandoned, I weep this

Hecuba
  miserable last hour

Andromache

           of the house where I bore my children.

Hecuba
  O my sons, this city and your mother are desolate of you.
  Sound of lamentation and sorrow,
  tears on tears shed. Home, farewell, since the dead have forgotten   605
  all sorrows, and weep no longer.

Chorus
  They who are sad find somehow sweetness in tears, the song
  of lamentation and the melancholy Muse.

Andromache
  Hecuba, mother of the man whose spear was death   610
  to the Argives, Hector: do you see what they have done to us?

Hecuba
  I see the work of gods who pile tower-high the pride
  of those who were nothing, and dash present grandeur down.

Andromache

We are carried away, sad spoils, my boy and I; our life
transformed, as the aristocrat becomes the serf.   615

Hecuba

Such is the terror of necessity. I lost
Cassandra, roughly torn from my arms before you came.

Andromache

Another Ajax to haunt your daughter? Some such thing
it must be. Yet you have lost still more than you yet know.

Hecuba

There is no numbering my losses. Infinitely   620
misfortune comes to outrace misfortune known before.

Andromache

Polyxena is dead. They cut your daughter's throat
to pleasure dead Achilles' corpse, above his grave.

Hecuba

O wretched. This was what Talthybius meant, that speech
cryptic, incomprehensible, yet now so clear.   625

Andromache

I saw her die, and left this wagon seat to lay
a robe upon her body and sing the threnody.

Hecuba

Poor child, poor wretched, wretched darling, sacrificed,
but without pity, and in pain, to a dead man.

Andromache

She is dead, and this was death indeed; and yet to die   630
as she did was better than to live as I live now.

Hecuba

Child, no. No life, no light is any kind of death,
since death is nothing, and in life the hopes live still.

Andromache

O Mother, our mother, hear me while I reason through
this matter fairly—might it even hush your grief?   635

Death, I am sure, is like never being born, but death
is better thus by far than to live a life of pain,
since the dead with no perception of evil feel no grief,
while he who was happy once, and then unfortunate,
finds his heart driven far from the old lost happiness.   640
She died; it is as if she never saw the light
of day, for she knows nothing now of what she suffered.
But I, who aimed the arrows of ambition high
at honor, and made them good, see now how far I fall,
I, who in Hector's house worked out all custom that brings   645
discretion's name to women. Blame them or blame them not,
there is one act that swings the scandalous speech their way
beyond all else: to leave the house and walk abroad.
I longed to do it, but put the longing aside, and stayed
always within the inclosure of my own house and court.   650
The witty speech some women cultivate I would
not practice, but kept my honest inward thought, and made
my mind my only and sufficient teacher. I gave
my lord's presence the tribute of hushed lips, and eyes
quietly downcast. I knew when my will must have its way   655
over his, knew also how to give way to him in turn.
Men learned of this; I was talked of in the Achaean camp,
and reputation has destroyed me now. At the choice
of women, Achilles' son picked me from the rest, to be
his wife: a lordly house, yet I shall be a slave.   660
If I dash back the beloved memory of Hector
and open wide my heart to my new lord, I shall be
a traitor to the dead love, and know it; if I cling
faithful to the past, I win my master's hatred. Yet
they say one night of love suffices to dissolve   665
a woman's aversion to share the bed of any man.
I hate and loathe that woman who casts away the once
beloved, and takes another in her arms of love.
Even the young mare torn from her running mate and teamed
with another will not easily wear the yoke. And yet   670
this is a brute and speechless beast of burden, not

like us intelligent, lower far in nature's scale.
Dear Hector, when I had you I had a husband, great
in understanding, rank, wealth, courage: all my wish.
I was a virgin when you took me from the house   675
of my father; I gave you all my maiden love, my first,
and now you are dead, and I must cross the sea, to serve,
prisoner of war, the slave's yoke on my neck, in Greece.
No, Hecuba; can you not see my fate is worse
than hers you grieve, Polyxena's? That one thing left   680
always while life lasts, hope, is not for me. I keep
no secret deception in my heart—sweet though it be
to dream—that I shall ever be happy any more.

Chorus

You stand where I do in misfortune, and while you mourn
your own life, tell me what I, too, am suffering.   685

Hecuba

I have never been inside the hull of a ship, but know
what I know only by hearsay and from painted scenes,
yet think that seamen, while the gale blows moderately,
take pains to spare unnecessary work, and send
one man to the steering oar, another aloft, and crews   690
to pump the bilge from the hold. But when the tempest comes,
and seas wash over the decks they lose their nerve, and let
her go by the run at the waves' will, leaving all to chance.
So I, in this succession of disasters, swamped,
battered by this storm immortally inspired, have lost   695
my lips' control and let them go, say anything
they will. Yet still, beloved child, you must forget
what happened with Hector. Tears will never save you now.
Give your obedience to the new master; let your ways
entice his heart to make him love you. If you do   700
it will be better for all who are close to you. This boy,
my own son's child, might grow to manhood and bring back—
he alone could do it—something of our city's strength.

On some far day the children of your children might
come home, and build. There still may be another Troy.   705

But *we* say this, and others will speak also. See,
here is some runner of the Achaeans come again.
Who is he? What news? What counsel have they taken now?

(*Talthybius enters again with his escort.*)

Talthybius
O wife of Hector, once the bravest man in Troy,
do not hate me. This is the will of the Danaans and   710
the kings. I wish I did not have to give this message.

Andromache
What can this mean, this hint of hateful things to come?

Talthybius
The council has decreed for your son—how can I say this?

Andromache
That he shall serve some other master than I serve?

Talthybius
No man of Achaea shall ever make this boy his slave.   715

Andromache
Must he be left behind in Phrygia, all alone?

Talthybius
Worse; horrible. There is no easy way to tell it.

Andromache
I thank your courtesy—unless your news be really good.

Talthybius
They will kill your son. It is monstrous. Now you know the truth.

Andromache
Oh, this is worse than anything I heard before.   720

Talthybius
Odysseus. He urged it before the Greeks, and got his way.

Andromache
This is too much grief, and more than anyone could bear.

« EURIPIDES »

Talthybius

He said a hero's son could not be allowed to live.

Andromache

Even thus may his own sons some day find no mercy.

Talthybius

He must be hurled from the battlements of Troy.

> (*He goes toward Andromache, who clings fast
> to her child, as if to resist.*)

No, wait!   725
Let it happen this way. It will be wiser in the end.
Do not fight it. Take your grief as you were born to take it,
give up the struggle where your strength is feebleness
with no force anywhere to help. Listen to me!
Your city is gone, your husband. You are in our power.   730
How can one woman hope to struggle against the arms
of Greece? Think, then. Give up the passionate contest.
This
will bring no shame. No man can laugh at your submission.
And please—I request you—hurl no curse at the Achaeans
for fear the army, savage over some reckless word,   735
forbid the child his burial and the dirge of honor.
Be brave, be silent; out of such patience you can hope
the child you leave behind will not lie unburied here,
and that to you the Achaeans will be less unkind.

Andromache

O darling child I loved too well for happiness,   740
your enemies will kill you and leave your mother forlorn.
Your own father's nobility, where others found
protection, means your murder now. The memory
of his valor comes ill-timed for you. O bridal bed,
O marriage rites that brought me home to Hector's house   745
a bride, you were unhappy in the end. I lived
never thinking the baby I had was born for butchery
by Greeks, but for lordship over all Asia's pride of earth.

Poor child, are you crying too? Do you know what they
will do to you? Your fingers clutch my dress. What use,   750
to nestle like a young bird under the mother's wing?
Hector cannot come back, not burst from underground
to save you, that spear of glory caught in the quick hand,
nor Hector's kin, nor any strength of Phrygian arms.
Yours the sick leap head downward from the height, the fall   755
where none have pity, and the spirit smashed out in death.
O last and loveliest embrace of all, O child's
sweet fragrant body. Vanity in the end. I nursed
for nothing the swaddled baby at this mother's breast;
in vain the wrack of the labor pains and the long sickness.   760
Now once again, and never after this, come close
to your mother, lean against my breast and wind your arms
around my neck, and put your lips against my lips.

(*She kisses Astyanax and relinquishes him.*)

Greeks! Your Greek cleverness is simple barbarity.
Why kill this child, who never did you any harm?   765
O flowering of the house of Tyndareus! Not his,
not God's daughter, never that, but child of many fathers
I say; the daughter of Vindictiveness, of Hate,
of Blood, Death; of all wickedness that swarms on earth.
I cry it aloud: Zeus never was your father, but you   770
were born a pestilence to all Greeks and the world beside.
Accursed; who from those lovely and accursed eyes
brought down to shame and ruin the bright plains of Troy.
Oh, seize him, take him, dash him to death if it must be done;
feed on his flesh if it is your will. These are the gods   775
who damn us to this death, and I have no strength to save
my boy from execution. Cover this wretched face
and throw me into the ship and that sweet bridal bed
I walk to now across the death of my own child.

(*Talthybius gently lifts the child out of the wagon, which
leaves the stage, carrying Andromache away.*)

Chorus

    Unhappy Troy! For the sweetness in one woman's arms'   780
    embrace, unspeakable, you lost these thousands slain.

Talthybius

    Come, boy, taken from the embrace beloved
    of your mourning mother. Climb the high circle
    of the walls your fathers built. There
    end life. This was the order.   785
    Take him.

            (He hands Astyanax to the guards, who lead him out.)
        I am not the man
    to do this. Some other
    without pity, not as I ashamed,
    should be herald of messages like this.

                      (He goes out.)

Hecuba

    O child of my own unhappy child,   790
    shall your life be torn from your mother
    and from me? Wicked. Can I help,
    dear child, not only suffer? What help?
    Tear face, beat bosom. This is all
    my power now. O city,   795
    O child, what have we left to suffer?
    Are we not hurled
    down the whole length of disaster?

Chorus

    Telamon, O king in the land where the bees swarm,
    Salamis the surf-pounded isle where you founded your city   800
    to front that hallowed coast where Athene broke
    forth the primeval pale branch of olive,
    wreath of the bright air and a glory on Athens the shining:
    O Telamon, you came in your pride of arms
    with Alcmena's archer   805
    to Ilium, our city, to sack and destroy it
    on that age-old venture.

This was the first flower of Hellenic strength Heracles brought
   in anger
for the horses promised; and by Simois' calm waters   810
checked the surf-wandering oars and made fast the ships' stern
   cables.
From which vessels came out the deadly bow hand,
death to Laomedon, as the scarlet wind of the flames swept over
masonry straight-hewn by the hands of Apollo.   815
This was a desolation of Troy
twice taken; twice in the welter of blood the walls Dardanian
went down before the red spear.

In vain, then, Laomedon's child,   820
you walk in delicate pride
by the golden pitchers
in loveliest servitude
to fill Zeus' wine cups;
while Troy your mother is given to the flame to eat,   825
and the lonely beaches
mourn, as sad birds sing
for the young lost,   830
for the sword hand and the children
and the aged women.
Gone now the shining pools where you bathed,
the fields where you ran
all desolate. And you,
Ganymede, go in grace by the thrones of God   835
with your young, calm smile even now
as Priam's kingdom
falls to the Greek spear.   840

O Love, Love, it was you
in the high halls of Dardanus,
the sky-daughters of melody beside you,
who piled the huge strength of Troy
in towers, the gods' own hands   845
concerned. I speak no more

against Zeus' name.
But the light men love, who shines
through the pale wings of morning,
balestar on this earth now,   850
watched the collapse of tall towers:
Dawn. Her lord was of this land;
she bore his children,
Tithonus, caught away by the golden car
and the starry horses,   855
who made our hopes so high.
For the gods loved Troy once.
Now they have forgotten.

(*Menelaus comes on the stage, attended by a detail of
armed soldiers.*)

Menelaus

O splendor of sunburst breaking forth this day, whereon   860
I lay my hands once more on Helen, my wife. And yet
it is not, so much as men think, for the woman's sake
I came to Troy, but against that guest proved treacherous,   865
who like a robber carried the woman from my house.
Since the gods have seen to it that *he* paid the penalty,
fallen before the Hellenic spear, his kingdom wrecked,
I come for *her* now, the wife once my own, whose name
I can no longer speak with any happiness,   870
to take her away. In this house of captivity
she is numbered among the other women of Troy, a slave.
And those men whose work with the spear has won her back
gave her to me, to kill, or not to kill, but lead
away to the land of Argos, if such be my pleasure.   875
And such it is; the death of Helen in Troy I will let
pass, have the oars take her by sea ways back to Greek
soil, and there give her over to execution;
blood penalty for friends who are dead in Ilium here.
Go to the house, my followers, and take her out;   880
no, drag her out; lay hands upon that hair so stained

with men's destruction. When the winds blow fair astern
we will take ship again and bring her back to Hellas.

Hecuba

O power, who mount the world, wheel where the world rides,
O mystery of man's knowledge, whosoever you be,   885
Zeus named, nature's necessity or mortal mind,
I call upon you; for you walk the path none hears
yet bring all human action back to right at last.

Menelaus

What can this mean? How strange a way to call on gods.

Hecuba

Kill your wife, Menelaus, and I will bless your name.   890
But keep your eyes away from her. Desire will win.
She looks enchantment, and where she looks homes are set fire;
she captures cities as she captures the eyes of men.
We have had experience, you and I. We know the truth.

> (*Men at arms bring Helen roughly out of the shelter.*
> *She makes no resistance.*)

Helen

Menelaus, your first acts are argument of terror   895
to come. Your lackeys put their hands on me. I am dragged
out of my chambers by brute force. I know you hate
me; I am almost sure. And still there is one question
I would ask you, if I may. What have the Greeks decided
to do with me? Or shall I be allowed to live?   900

Menelaus

You are not strictly condemned, but all the army gave
you into my hands, to kill you for the wrong you did.

Helen

Is it permitted that I argue this, and prove
that my death, if I am put to death, will be unjust?

Menelaus

I did not come to talk with you. I came to kill.   905

Hecuba

No, Menelaus, listen to her. She should not die
unheard. But give me leave to take the opposite case;
the prosecution. There are things that happened in Troy
which you know nothing of, and the long-drawn argument
will mean her death. She never can escape us now.   910

Menelaus

This is a gift of leisure. If she wishes to speak
she may. But it is for your sake, understand, that I give
this privilege I never would have given to her.

Helen

Perhaps it will make no difference if I speak well
or badly, and your hate will not let you answer me.   915
All I can do is to foresee the arguments
you will use in accusation of me, and set against
the force of your charges, charges of my own.

                                                          First, then!
She mothered the beginning of all this wickedness.
For Paris was her child. And next to her the old king,   920
who would not destroy the infant Alexander, that dream
of the firebrand's agony, has ruined Troy, and me.
This is not all; listen to the rest I have to say.
Alexander was the judge of the goddess trinity.
Pallas Athene would have given him power, to lead   925
the Phrygian arms on Hellas and make it desolate.
All Asia was Hera's promise, and the uttermost zones
of Europe for his lordship, if her way prevailed.
But Aphrodite, picturing my loveliness,
promised it to him, if he would say her beauty surpassed   930
all others. Think what this means, and all the consequence.
Cypris prevailed, and I was won in marriage: all
for Greek advantage. Asia is not your lord; you serve
no tyrant now, nor take the spear in his defense.
Yet Hellas' fortune was my own misfortune. I,   935

sold once for my body's beauty stand accused, who should
for what has been done wear garlands on my head.

                                      I know.

You will say all this is nothing to the immediate charge:
I did run away; I did go secretly from your house.
But when he came to me—call him any name you will: 940
Paris? or Alexander? or the spirit of blood
to haunt this woman?—he came with a goddess at his side;
no weak one. And you—it was criminal—took ship for Crete
and left me there in Sparta in the house, alone.

You see?

I wonder—and I ask this of myself, not you—   945
why *did* I do it? What made me run away from home
with the stranger, and betray my country and my hearth?
Challenge the goddess then, show your greater strength than
    Zeus'
who has the other gods in his power, and still is slave
to Aphrodite alone. Shall I not be forgiven?   950
Still you might have some show of argument against me.
When Paris was gone to the deep places of death, below
ground, and the immortal practice on my love was gone,
I should have come back to the Argive ships, left Troy.
I did try to do it, and I have witnesses,   955
the towers' gatekeepers and the sentinels on the wall,
who caught me again and again as I let down the rope
from the battlements and tried to slip away to the ground.
For Deiphobus, my second husband: he took me away
by force and kept me his wife against the Phrygians' will.   960

O my husband, can you kill me now and think you kill
in righteousness? I was the bride of force. Before,
I brought their houses to the sorrow of slavery
instead of conquest. Would you be stronger than the gods?
Try, then. But even such ambition is absurd.   965

Chorus

> O Queen of Troy, stand by your children and your country!
> Break down the beguilement of this woman, since she speaks
> well, and has done wickedly. This is dangerous.

Hecuba

> First, to defend the honor of the gods, and show
> that the woman is a scandalous liar. I will not   970
> believe it! Hera and the virgin Pallas Athene
> could never be so silly and empty-headed
> that Hera would sell Argos to the barbarians,
> or Pallas let Athenians be the slaves of Troy.
> They went to Ida in girlish emulation, vain   975
> of their own loveliness? Why? Tell me the reason Hera
> should fall so much in love with the idea of beauty.
> To win some other lord more powerful than Zeus?
> Or has Athene marked some god to be her mate,
> she, whose virginity is a privilege won from Zeus,   980
> who abjures marriage? Do not trick out your own sins
> by calling the gods stupid. No wise man will believe you.
> You claim, and I must smile to hear it, that Aphrodite
> came at my son's side to the house of Menelaus;
> who could have caught up you and your city of Amyclae   985
> and set you in Ilium, moving not from the quiet of heaven.
> Nonsense. My son was handsome beyond all other men.
> You looked at him, and sense went Cyprian at the sight,
> since Aphrodite is nothing but the human lust,
> named rightly, since the word of lust begins the god's name.   990
> You saw him in the barbaric splendor of his robes,
> gorgeous with gold. It made your senses itch. You thought,
> being queen only in Argos, in little luxury,
> that once you got rid of Sparta for the Phrygian city
> where gold streamed everywhere, you could let extravagance   995
> run wild. No longer were Menelaus and his house
> sufficient to your spoiled luxurious appetites.

So much for that. You say my son took you away
by force. What Spartan heard you cry for help? You did
cry out? Or did you? Castor, your brother, was there, a young   1000
man, and his twin not yet caught up among the stars.
Then when you had reached Troy, and the Argives at your heels
came, and the agony of the murderous spears began,
when the reports came in that Menelaus' side
was winning, you would praise him, simply to make my son   1005
unhappy at the strength of his love's challenger,
forgetting your husband when the luck went back to Troy.
You worked hard: not to make yourself a better woman,
but to make sure always to be on the winning side.
You claim you tried to slip away with ropes let down   1010
from the ramparts, and this proves you stayed against your will?
Perhaps. But when were you ever caught in the strangling noose,
caught sharpening a dagger? Which any noble wife
would do, desperate with longing for her lord's return.
Yet over and over again I gave you good advice: 1015
"Make your escape, my daughter; there are other girls
for my sons to marry. I will help you get away
to the ships of the Achaeans. Let the Greeks, and us,
stop fighting." So I argued, but you were not pleased.
Spoiled in the luxury of Alexander's house   1020
you liked foreigners to kiss the ground before your feet.
All that impressed you.

              And now you dare to come outside,
figure fastidiously arranged, to look upon
the same air as your husband, O abominable
heart, who should walk submissively in rags of robes,   1025
shivering with anxiety, head Scythian-cropped,
your old impudence gone and modesty gained at last
by reason of your sinful life.

              O Menelaus,
mark this, the end of my argument. Be true to your
high reputation and to Hellas. Grace both, and kill   1030

Helen. Thus make it the custom toward all womankind
hereafter, that the price of adultery is death.

Chorus

Menelaus, keep the ancestral honor of your house.
Punish your wife, and purge away from Greece the stigma
on women. You shall seem great even to your enemies.   1035

Menelaus

All you have said falls into line with my own thought.
This woman left my household for a stranger's bed
of her own free will, and all this talk of Aphrodite
is for pure show. Away, and face the stones of the mob.
Atone for the long labors of the Achaeans in   1040
the brief act of dying, and know your penance for my shame.

(Helen drops before him and embraces his knees.)

Helen

No, by your knees! I am not guilty of the mind's
infection, which the gods sent. Do not kill! Have pity!

Hecuba

Be true to the memory of all your friends she murdered.
It is for them and for their children that I plead.   1045

(Menelaus pushes Helen away.)

Menelaus

Enough, Hecuba. I am not listening to her now.
I speak to my servants: see that she is taken away
to where the ships are beached. She will make the voyage home.

Hecuba

But let her not be put in the same ship with you.

Menelaus

What can you mean? That she is heavier than she was?   1050

Hecuba

A man in love once never is out of love again.

Menelaus

Sometimes; when the beloved's heart turns false to him.
Yet it shall be as you wish. She shall not be allowed

in the same ship I sail in. This was well advised.
And once in Argos she must die the vile death earned   1055
by her vile life, and be an example to all women
to live temperately. This is not the easier way;
and yet her execution will tincture with fear
the lust of women even more depraved than she.

(*Helen is led out, Menelaus following.*)

Chorus

Thus, O Zeus, you betrayed all   1060
to the Achaeans: your temple
in Ilium, your misted altar,
the flame of the clotted sacraments,
the smoke of the skying incense,
Pergamum the hallowed,   1065
the ivied ravines of Ida, washed
by the running snow. The utter
peaks that surprise the sun bolts,
shining and primeval place of divinity.   1070

Gone are your sacrifices, the choirs'
glad voices singing to the gods
night long, deep into darkness;
gone the images, gold on wood
laid, the twelves of the sacred moons,   1075
the magic Phrygian number.
Can it be, can it be, my lord, you have forgotten
from your throne high in heaven's
bright air, my city which is ruined
and the flame storm that broke it?   1080

O my dear, my husband,
O wandering ghost
unwashed, unburied; the sea hull must carry me   1085
in the flash of its wings' speed
to Argos, city of horses, where
the stone walls built by giants invade the sky.   1090
The multitudes of our children stand

clinging to the gates and cry through their tears.
And one girl weeps:
"O Mother, the Achaeans take me away
lonely from your eyes
to the black ship
where the oars dip surf   1095
toward Salamis the blessed,
or the peak between two seas
where Pelops' hold
keeps the gates at the Isthmus."

Oh that as Menelaus' ship   1100
makes way through the mid-sea
the bright pronged spear immortal of thunder might smash it
far out in the Aegaean,
as in tears, in bondage to Hellas   1105
I am cut from my country;
as she holds the golden mirror
in her hands, girls' grace,
she, God's daughter.
Let him never come home again, to a room in Laconia   1110
and the hearth of his fathers;
never more to Pitana's streets
and the bronze gates of the Maiden;
since he forgave his shame
and the vile marriage, the sorrows   1115
of great Hellas and the land
watered by Simois.

       *(Talthybius returns. His men carry, laid on the shield of
                      Hector, the body of Astyanax.)*

But see!
Now evils multiply in our land.
Behold, O pitiful wives
of the Trojans. This is Astyanax,   1120
dead, dashed without pity from the walls, and borne
by the Danaans, who murdered him.

Talthybius

    Hecuba, one last vessel of Achilles' son
remains, manned at the oar sweeps now, to carry back
to the shores of Phthiotis his last spoils of war.   1125
Neoptolemus himself has put to sea. He heard
news of old Peleus in difficulty and the land
invaded by Acastus, son of Pelias.
Such news put speed above all pleasure of delay.
So he is gone, and took with him Andromache,   1130
whose lamentations for her country and farewells
to Hector's tomb as she departed brought these tears
crowding into my eyes. And she implored that you
bury this dead child, your own Hector's son, who died
flung from the battlements of Troy. She asked as well   1135
that the bronze-backed shield, terror of the Achaeans once,
when the boy's father slung its defense across his side,
be not taken to the hearth of Peleus, nor the room
where the slain child's Andromache must be a bride
once more, to waken memories by its sight, but used   1140
in place of the cedar coffin and stone-chambered tomb
for the boy's burial. He shall be laid in your arms
to wrap the body about with winding sheets, and flowers,
as well as you can, out of that which is left to you.
Since she is gone. Her master's speed prevented her   1145
from giving the rites of burial to her little child.

    The rest of us, once the corpse is laid out, and earth
is piled above it, must raise the mast tree, and go.
Do therefore quickly everything that you must do.
There is one labor I myself have spared you. As   1150
we forded on our way here Scamander's running water,
I washed the body and made clean the wounds. I go
now, to break ground and dig the grave for him, that my
work be made brief, as yours must be, and our tasks end
together, and the ships be put to sea, for home.   1155

Hecuba

    Lay down the circled shield of Hector on the ground:
a hateful thing to look at; it means no love to me.

        (Talthybius and his escort leave. Two soldiers wait.)

    Achaeans! All your strength is in your spears, not in
the mind. What were you afraid of, that it made you kill
this child so savagely? That Troy, which fell, might be   1160
raised from the ground once more? Your strength meant
   nothing, then.
When Hector's spear was fortunate, and numberless
strong hands were there to help him, we were still destroyed.
Now when the city is fallen and the Phrygians slain,
this baby terrified you? I despise the fear   1165
which is pure terror in a mind unreasoning.

    O darling child, how wretched was this death. You might
have fallen fighting for your city, grown to man's
age, and married, and with the king's power like a god's,
and died happy, if there is any happiness here.   1170
But no. You grew to where you could see and learn, my child,
yet your mind was not old enough to win advantage
of fortune. How wickedly, poor boy, your fathers' walls,
Apollo's handiwork, have crushed your pitiful head
tended and trimmed to ringlets by your mother's hand,   1175
and the face she kissed once, where the brightness now is blood
shining through the torn bones—too horrible to say more.
O little hands, sweet likenesses of Hector's once,
now you lie broken at the wrists before my feet;
and mouth beloved whose words were once so confident,   1180
you are dead; and all was false, when you would lean across
my bed, and say: "Mother, when you die I will cut
my long hair in your memory, and at your grave
bring companies of boys my age, to sing farewell."
It did not happen; now I, a homeless, childless, old   1185
woman must bury your poor corpse, which is so young.
Alas for all the tendernesses, my nursing care,

and all your slumbers gone. What shall the poet say,
what words will he inscribe upon your monument?
Here lies a little child the Argives killed, because　　　　1190
they were afraid of him. That? The epitaph of Greek shame.
You will not win your father's heritage, except
for this, which is your coffin now: the brazen shield.

O shield, who guarded the strong shape of Hector's arm:
the bravest man of all, who wore you once, is dead.　　　　1195
How sweet the impression of his body on your sling,
and at the true circle of your rim the stain of sweat
where in the grind of his many combats Hector leaned
his chin against you, and the drops fell from his brow!

Take up your work now; bring from what is left some robes　　　1200
to wrap the tragic dead. The gods will not allow us
to do it right. But let him have what we can give.

That mortal is a fool who, prospering, thinks his life
has any strong foundation; since our fortune's course
of action is the reeling way a madman takes,　　　　1205
and no one person is ever happy all the time.

> (*Hecuba's handmaidens bring out from the shelter a basket of
> robes and ornaments. During the scene which follows,
> the body of Astyanax is being made ready for burial.*)

Chorus

Here are your women, who bring you from the Trojan spoils
such as is left, to deck the corpse for burial.

Hecuba

O child, it is not for victory in riding, won
from boys your age, not archery—in which acts our people　　　1210
take pride, without driving competition to excess—
that your sire's mother lays upon you now these treasures
from what was yours before; though now the accursed of God,
Helen, has robbed you, she who has destroyed as well
the life in you, and brought to ruin all our house.　　　　1215

Chorus

    My heart,
    you touched my heart, you who were once
    a great lord in my city.

Hecuba

    These Phrygian robes' magnificence you should have worn
    at your marriage to some princess uttermost in pride
    in all the East, I lay upon your body now.   1220
    And you, once so victorious and mother of
    a thousand conquests, Hector's huge beloved shield:
    here is a wreath for you, who die not, yet are dead
    with this body; since it is better far to honor you
    than the armor of Odysseus the wicked and wise.   1225

Chorus

    Ah me.
    Earth takes you, child;
    our tears of sorrow.
    Cry aloud, our mother.

Hecuba

                Yes.

Chorus

    The dirge of the dead.

Hecuba

               Ah me.   1230

Chorus

    Evils never to be forgotten.

Hecuba

    I will bind up your wounds with bandages, and be
    your healer: a wretched one, in name alone, no use.
    Among the dead your father will take care of you.

Chorus

    Rip, tear your faces with hands   1235
    that beat like oars.
    Alas.

Hecuba

Dear women. . . .

Chorus

Hecuba, speak to us. We are yours. What did you cry aloud?

Hecuba

The gods meant nothing except to make life hard for me,   1240
and of all cities they chose Troy to hate. In vain
we sacrificed. And yet had not the very hand
of God gripped and crushed this city deep in the ground,
we should have disappeared in darkness, and not given
a theme for music, and the songs of men to come.   1245
You may go now, and hide the dead in his poor tomb;
he has those flowers that are the right of the underworld.
I think it makes small difference to the dead, if they
are buried in the tokens of luxury. All this
is an empty glorification left for those who live.   1250

*(The soldiers take up and carry away the body
of Astyanax.)*

Chorus

Sad mother, whose hopes were so huge
for your life. They are broken now.
Born to high blessedness
and a lordly line
your death was horror.   1255

But see, see
on the high places of Ilium
the torchflares whirling in the hands
of men. For Troy
some ultimate agony.

(Talthybius comes back, with numerous men.)

Talthybius

I call to the captains who have orders to set fire   1260
to the city of Priam: shield no longer in the hand
the shining flame. Let loose the fire upon it. So

with the citadel of Ilium broken to the ground
we can take leave of Troy, in gladness, and go home.

I speak to you, too, for my orders include this.   1265
Children of Troy, when the lords of the armament sound
the high echoing crash of the trumpet call, then go
to the ships of the Achaeans, to be taken away
from this land. And you, unhappiest and aged woman,
go with them. For Odysseus' men are here, to whom   1270
enslaved the lot exiles you from your native land.

Hecuba

Ah, wretched me. So this is the unhappy end
and goal of all the sorrows I have lived. I go
forth from my country and a city lit with flames.
Come, aged feet; make one last weary struggle, that I   1275
may hail my city in its affliction. O Troy, once
so huge over all Asia in the drawn wind of pride,
your very name of glory shall be stripped away.
They are burning you, and us they drag forth from our land
enslaved. O gods! Do I call upon those gods for help?   1280
I cried to them before now, and they would not hear.
Come then, hurl ourselves into the pyre. Best now
to die in the flaming ruins of our fathers' house!

Talthybius

Unhappy creature, ecstatic in your sorrows! Men,
take her, spare not. She is Odysseus' property.   1285
You have orders to deliver her into his hands.

Hecuba

O sorrow.
Cronion, Zeus, lord of Phrygia,
prince of our house, have you seen
the dishonor done to the seed of Dardanus?   1290

Chorus

He has seen, but the great city
is a city no more, it is gone. There is no Troy.

Hecuba

   O sorrow.
   Ilium flares.   1295
   The chambers of Pergamum take fire,
   the citadel and the wall's high places.

Chorus

   Our city fallen to the spear
   fades as smoke winged in the sky.
   halls hot in the swept fire   1300
   and the fierce lances.

Hecuba

   O soil where my children grew.

Chorus

   Alas.

Hecuba

   O children, hear me; it is your mother who calls.

Chorus

   They are dead you cry to. This is a dirge.

Hecuba

   I lean my old body against the earth   1305
   and both hands beat the ground.

Chorus

   I kneel to the earth, take up
   the cry to my own dead,
   poor buried husband.

Hecuba

   We are taken, dragged away

Chorus

                                a cry of pain, pain   1310

Hecuba

   under the slave's roof

Chorus

                       away from my country.

Hecuba

    Priam, my Priam. Dead
    graveless, forlorn,
    you know not what they have done to me.

Chorus

    Now dark, holy death   1315
    in the brutal butchery closed his eyes.

Hecuba

    O gods' house, city beloved

Chorus

    alas

Hecuba

    you are given the red flame and the spear's iron.

Chorus

    You will collapse to the dear ground and be nameless.

Hecuba

    Ash as the skyward smoke wing   1320
    piled will blot from my sight the house where I lived once.

Chorus

    Lost shall be the name on the land,
    all gone, perished. Troy, city of sorrow,
    is there no longer.

Hecuba

    Did you see, did you hear?

Chorus

                    The crash of the citadel.   1325

Hecuba

    The earth shook, riven

Chorus

                  to engulf the city.

Hecuba

    O
    shaking, tremulous limbs,

this is the way. Forward:
into the slave's life.   1330

Chorus
Mourn for the ruined city, then go away
to the ships of the Achaeans.

> (*Hecuba is led away, and all go out, leaving
> the stage empty.*)